E N

Ron Luce and the
major issues of concern facing the church in the twenty —
—bringing teenagers to Christ and engagement in his church. This
manual reflects the best of church growth practice and wisdom
gleaned from experience, sociology, business and the insight of
Scripture. I strongly recommend its use.

Berten A. Waggoner, National Director
Vineyard Churches USA

A new generation of men and women are waiting to be inspired to
something so large that they can't get their teeth around it. And just
like the needle of a compass that is drawn toward true north, Ron
Luce's book provides substance that will inspire the youth of today's
generation to be pointed directly toward God. If it matters to you
that your life and those whom you lead are headed in the right direction, then Ron Luce's book is a must read.

John E. Zuch, Executive Director for Church Ministries
The Christian and Missionary Alliance

WOW, Ron Luce hits a home run with this one! From rethinking as
a youth volunteer or pastor to seeing one's self as a Youth Specialist;
becoming a leader who has vision, a dream, and casting that vision
before his/her people; having a plan and working the plan and actually working the plan into a reality—this is a must read for all those
in leadership who work with youth.

Pete White, Student Ministries Coordinator
General Baptist Ministries

It is practical and principle-laden. This is not another "cookie-cutter"
youth ministry manual. The principles shared will dramatically
assist someone who is just starting in youth ministry while it helps
the seasoned youth ministers to rekindle their passion for their purpose and fine tune their ministry.

Steve Ely, National Youth Director
International Pentecostal Holiness Church

Ron Luce has done an excellent job of not only identifying a major
problem facing the world today, but has laid out a plan to deal with
this crisis. A must read.

Thomas J. Usher, CEO
U.S. Steel Corp

DOUBLE VISION

– BUILDING A PLAN FOR HIGH IMPACT YOUTH MINISTRY –

RONLUCE

DOUBLE VISION VOL. 2

Double Vision — Having a Plan for High Impact Youth Ministry
Published by TM Publishing, a division of Teen Mania Ministries
22392 FM 16 West Garden Valley, TX 75771
www.teenmania.org

ISBN 978-1-936417-04-9
© 2010 Ron Luce

Printed in the United States of America

RELIGION / CHRISTIAN MINISTRY / YOUTH

DEDICATION

This book is dedicated to those who
have poured their guts out for this
generation.

ACKNOWLEDGMENTS

The Double Vision book series is the effort of many people's time and energy. I would like to acknowledge a few of those individuals.

Thank you to my Executive Team, Beth Powell, Rebekah Morris, Emily Johnson, Heidi Abigt, Laurie Fields, and LauRen Spillers. Thank you for all the work you do to keep things flowing and for all the hours that you put into making this book possible.

This book series would be meaningless without all the Youth Pastors and Youth Workers in the world. If you are a Youth Pastor or Youth Worker, I want to thank you for the time, blood, sweat, tears, and pizza you have gone through to reach this generation.

I have to acknowledge my amazing children Hannah, Charity, and Cameron. My wife of over 25 years, Katie, you are a wonderful wife, mother, and best friend.

Finally, John 15:5 says, *"I am the vine, you are the branches. . . without Me you can do nothing"* (NKJV). My life is nothing without the Lord. There aren't enough words in all the books in all the world to express how thankful I am to You.

C O N T E N T S

Letter to You From Ron Luce 9

Introduction 11

Chapter 1 Plan to Turn Your Dreams into Reality 13

Chapter 2 BHAGs: Defining Them and Going For It 27

Chapter 3 Organizing and Managing the Plan 43

Chapter 4 Inventing the Future 57

Chapter 5 Funding Your Plan 71

Chapter 6 Building Your Dream Team 89

Chapter 7 Leading Your Dream Team 109

Chapter 8 Preparing for the Rollout 123

Chapter 9 The Ongoing Role of the Youth Specialist 137

Chapter 10 Preempting Problems as You Grow 149

Dear Youth Leader,

We are in the middle of a battle for the hearts of a whole generation. If you are like most youth leaders in America, you are in the trenches every day. You're wearing yourself out trying to do whatever you can to love kids, lead them to Christ, and help them grow. Even with all that's done in the name of youth ministry, we are still losing a generation. It seems like the media and the enemy have been working harder than we have. They are destroying a generation at a faster rate than we are rescuing it. At current rates of evangelism, only four percent of this generation will be Bible-believing Christian adults. If we continue doing youth ministry the way we have been, we will end up with an America unlike any we have ever known. Something has to change!

What you have in your hands is more than a book series. This is a manual to provoke a revolution in communities, churches, and youth ministries across America. If we want to capture the heart of this generation before it's too late, we need thousands of youth ministries and groups to double and disciple every year. *Double Vision* will help you to build a thriving, solid youth ministry that continues to flourish and grow without burning you out.

This book series and its accompanying CD-ROM are embedded with proven strategies and principles for building a thriving youth ministry. Already, thousands of youth pastors across the country are seeing God work powerfully through these new paradigms!

I encourage you to begin to dream God's dream for you in youth ministry. Could you be one of the 100,000 youth groups needed to capture the hearts of this generation? I believe if we all throw our hearts into this, work hard, work smart, and ask the Holy Spirit to guide us, we can win this war! We need to have drastic change . . . it has to start now . . . it has to start with us.

I look forward to laboring with you and thousands of other youth pastors of every denomination and background. I believe we will see a miracle in the hearts of this generation!

Consumed by the Call,

Ron Luce

President and Founder
Teen Mania Ministries

INTRODUCTION

You have in your hands a document of war—a blueprint for strategic thinking about your local youth ministry. It is meant to help you launch a local offensive in your region to rescue teens caught in the middle of the current war for their hearts and minds. It is meant to provoke a revolution in youth ministry.

We must come to grips with the fact that—in spite of all of our best efforts to minister to young people—we are on the brink of losing a generation! The world and the enemy have been working harder, investing millions, and gaining more ground than we have. We cannot simply do more of the same old things and hope to turn this generation around. We must change what we are doing. We must change how we think about youth ministry before it is too late.

What do I mean by too late? First, consider the numbers: the millennial generation is the largest and richest generation in American history. Every year, 4.5 million American teenagers turn 20, and research shows that the odds against someone turning to Christ after reaching this milestone are significant. (We know that 77 percent of people who receive Christ do so before they are 21 years old). At the present rate of evangelism, only four percent of this generation will be Bible-believing—so we must act NOW to prevent them from going into their adult years as unbelievers.[1] Our passion is fueled by the fact that in five to seven years MOST of this generation will be in their 20s. NOW is the time to capture their hearts.

With the urgency of the moment fresh in our minds, let us approach youth ministry with a new perspective. It is time to shift our focus off of maintaining ministry the way it's always been done—the weekly meetings, our regular programs, ski trips and bake sales. What will capture the critical mass of the youth in any region is a vision-driven, not program-driven, local youth ministry. And that is where you come in!

Those of us engaged in youth ministry need to redefine our job descriptions. In this war for today's generation, we are the generals. Wars are won by the generals in the field, and those generals must have a plan to win each battle. That is what this book is all about—a new paradigm that leads to a different kind of planning and a new way of executing local youth ministry.

Don't be intimidated by the size of this book series, or get weary in the planning process. You are invited to use the text of this guide with the included CD-ROM as a tool for the battle-planning process. These steps are the work of generals that are determined to win. Let us all commit ourselves to becoming generals.

1. The Barna Group, "Research Shows that Spiritual Maturity Process Should Start at a Young Age," (November 17, 2003) http://www.barna.org/FlexPage.aspx?Page=BarnaUpdate&BarnaUpdateID=153

CHAPTER ONE

Plan to Turn Your Dreams into Reality

I haven't always been the kind of planner that I am now. In the early days of ministry, I was much more focused on the end result (seeing people's lives transformed by the power of God) than on how to get there.

Does that ring true for you too? I know we all want to be flexible, creative, and open to the leading of the Holy Spirit. But can't the Spirit just as easily lead you in advance so that you can better plan how it should be done? Of course! There are many good reasons to plan.

You may dream big, but you'll never do something big unless you have a plan to get there.

WHY PLAN?

God is a planner. Do you think God created the universe without thinking it through first? Do you think He creates any one of us on a spur-of-the-moment whim? Somehow, I never really thought that God planned ahead. He does, in fact. We saw earlier that God planned Jeremiah's ministry before he was even born (Jer. 1:5). Revelation 13:8 says that before the foundation of the world, Jesus Christ was crucified. *Now that is planning in advance!* Let's give up excuses about our lack of planning and take a giant step toward becoming more like God. God is a planner.

You'll never do something big without a plan. You may dream big, but you'll never do something big unless you have a plan to get there. Too many people never realize their big dreams because they never make a big plan. Their unrealized dreams are a source of never-ending frustration.

God has blessed us here at Teen Mania. We had our first teen stadium event with 73,000 people. We've expanded the number of buildings on our campus. Our intern program and global missions have grown. This is absolutely a sign of God's grace, but a lot of people also worked, sweated, and planned those things for years to make them happen.

Again, we see the synergy of God's favor and your labor (in this case, planning labor). Few youth pastors are lazy. You're willing to work hard—but are you willing to do the right kind of work? Are you willing to plan when no one is cheering you on? This is the work of a leader.

It turns your dreams into reality. As great as dreams are, it's even greater to see them turned into reality. Dreams that stay dreams soon become regrets. God has sparked huge ideas in your heart! Plan them into reality.

It makes your dream seem possible and believable. When you plan, dreams become realistic. Planning shows what steps you have to take for the dream to become reality. Some of you may argue that you already have it laid out in your head. That's not enough! Not only do *you* need to know your plan, your people need to see how your dream may be possible. The plan—the vision—is for your kids, the people in your church, your pastor, and your adult volunteers. They need to know that you are not just carried along by a pie-in-the-sky whim. They need to think your dream is doable, and a step-by-step process shows them that. As you plan with them, talk through the process you've envisioned. Suddenly, they will begin to say, "You know what? We really can do this!" *As you plan, it makes the dream believable.*

I am not really a natural planner or a natural leader. But I learned that planning is the work of a leader. It won't bring you glory and most people will never see it, but that is what a leader does. Planning is how a leader becomes productive. One day, people will look at you and say, "Wow! You are reaching a lot of kids," and they'll think you're a really terrific leader because of what they see. You'll know it was the planning in advance that made it possible to reach all those students, not what happened up on stage. Don't feel bad if you are not a natural leader or planner. I learned it and so can you!

Dreams that stay dreams soon become regrets.

DOUBLED IN SIZE

Our youth group exploded! We doubled in size in one
year by following the teachings in [Double Vision].

—John, Youth Specialist

HOW TO PLAN

Step 1: The Mission Statement

What is it and why do I need one? Every world-class
organization has a mission statement. A mission statement
is a one- or two-sentence synopsis of your goals. It clarifies
your dream and focuses people on the real aim of your ministry. Here are some characteristics of a good mission statement:

- **It's short.** Take your dream and turn it into a
  two-sentence piece of fire. It is a high-impact synopsis of what is burning within you.

- **It's fun to say.** Make sure your mission statement
  rolls off the tongue. The result is that every time
  anyone says it, they get fired up about your
  dream. It should make you feel exhilarated:
  "Yahoo! I am glad I am doing this!"

- **It's specific.** It should be unique to your vision.
  It's too general to say, "We want to reach teens."
  It should say something about what kids you
  want to reach, how you want to reach them, and
  what you want to *see them become.*

Assemble the thoughts you want to include in your mission statement, then refine them to include only the most important ones. Wordsmith those ideas so they're concise and meaningful. You're building your whole plan on this statement; it's worth getting it right. Take your dream, boil it down, and then boil it down again to a few potent words.

Involve your pastor in the process to make sure your mission statement is in line with the mission statement of the church (or at least doesn't contradict). Some may say that you should ask your kids what the mission statement should be. No! That is why *you* are the leader. The leader goes to God and says, "God, what is your vision?" Then the leader brings it to his kids, saying, "This is what God has called us to." Moses didn't ask for the Israelites' input on the Ten Commandments or whether they should really head for the promised land.

Too many youth ministries have been run that way. Does that mean you should never seek input from students? No. You frequently seek their input, but you *don't let them drive who you are, your mission, or your purpose!* You can get input from them later in the planning process on *how* to do certain parts of the vision, but *what* the vision is must come from you the leader, as God lays it on your heart.

How do you use your mission statement?

Put it everywhere. Since this statement describes your heart and ministry you will want to put it on everything. Put it on your business cards (if you don't have cards you should make some). Put it on the banner behind your stage

Take your dream, boil it down, and then boil it down again to a few potent words.

Kids want to belong to something, and a mission statement helps them to belong to the ministry God has given you.

in the youth room. Put it on T-shirts, so everybody under-stands who you are and what you're all about. Use it every chance you get.

Clarify identity. Why is a mission statement so impor-tant? The group gains its identity from a mission statement. They already know the group name; the statement tells them what the name represents. For example, if your name is Wildfire, and everywhere they see the logo for Wildfire they see the mission statement, there is an instant burst of understanding. When they read, "Wildfire stands for _____!" they'll instantly be reminded of who they are.

Line everything up with it. Now use your mission state-ment to evaluate everything you do in your youth ministry. Anything you do must line up with your mission statement. After all, this is the pulse of what is beating inside of you. You must not waste your efforts on any activity, retreat, con-ference, concert, or camp that comes outside the span of this mission statement. Harness all your efforts to it.

One of the reasons you are so busy is that *you do so many things that have nothing to do with your purpose.* Yes, they are good activities, but if they don't move your purpose forward, they need to be stopped (at least some of them). Otherwise, they'll distract you from doing God's specific work. A mission statement should become the litmus test for all your youth ministry plans. Everything you do must pass or it shouldn't become part of your youth program.

Bring purpose to every worker. Every teen who attends your group should know your mission statement. They should be able to see how every activity fits into the mission. At Teen Mania, everybody knows the mission statement:

> *Our Heartbeat is . . . to provoke a young generation to passionately pursue Jesus Christ and to take His life-giving message to the ends of the earth!*

Every intern and staff member here is a part of this—if you ever come here, stop and ask any one of them. Each person understands how his or her job is connected to the mission. The guy mowing the lawn is more than just mowing the lawn—he's providing an environment of first-class excellence to help bring the life-giving message of Jesus to the ends of the earth.

If people don't feel part of something big, or see how their job fits into the mission statement, then they have very low motivation. At Teen Mania, kids don't just lick stamps. They realize they are helping to reach every kid in the country, so they get excited about their part of the outreach! The mission statement fuels them. It brings them identity! Kids want to belong to something, and a mission statement helps them to belong to the ministry God has given you.

Just about every secular company has some type of mission or vision statement:

- The goal of Robert Woodruff, President of Coca-Cola, is to have "every person in the world taste Coca-Cola."
- Wal-Mart wants "to give ordinary folk the chance to buy the same things as rich people."[1]
- 3M aims "to solve unsolved problems innovatively."[2]

A mission statement should become the litmus test for all your youth ministry plans.

- In the early 1900s, the Ford Motor Company set out to "democratize the automobile."[3]

The challenge for Christians is to meet or surpass their vision and purpose.

Your mission statement needs to be narrow enough to define who you are, but broad enough not to limit you. A mission statement should define exactly who you are. For example, Disney's mission statement doesn't say, "We want to make great cartoons." It says they want to "make people happy" through "creativity, dreams, and imagination."[4] They started with cartoons, but then expanded into Disneyland, Disney World, and other media which provide entertainment.

Let me give you some examples from a few youth ministries:

- *3-D Ministry in Norman, Oklahoma:*
  "We exist to direct young people of the Norman area to discover their identity in Christ Jesus, to develop a life-changing relationship with Him, and to demonstrate a life of integrity to others."
- *Upper Room Fellowship in Maryland:*
  "Our youth ministry department exists to glorify God through worship, serve Him through ministry, serve His world through evangelism, and strengthen others in Christ through fellowship and developing our faith in Christ through discipleship."

- *North Bay Christian Center in Mobile, Alabama:* "Somewhere to go, someone to know, something to do."

Stop now and go to the CD-ROM file titled "Why Plan" and start writing and refining your own mission statement. Teen Mania's mission statement is given as an example to help you. This is the beginning of the planning stage. It is the foundation for everything else.

Step 2: Core Values

The personality of your ministry. Your mission statement and core values are the two pillars that you build your ministry upon. They work in tandem. The mission statement declares *what* you are going to do, while your core values decide *how* you are going to do it. How you are going to carry yourself as you do those things? The core values are your ministry's character.

But what does that have to do with youth groups? Because you have a distinct culture in your youth group. In other words, what is the normal way that your kids act with each other? That is your *corporate culture*, or your youth group culture.

Your mission statement needs to be narrow enough to define who you are, but broad enough not to limit you.

Core values steer your culture. When you don't develop your own core values, you have a culture that is made up of values from somewhere else.

Core values steer your culture. When you don't develop your own core values, you have a culture that is made up of values from somewhere else. You get it by default. Core values describe how you act.

Why is this so important? Let me tell you why by using the example of Teen Mania. Teen Mania used to be a place where people didn't like to work (including me). Our corporate culture was terrible. I couldn't figure out how to make it better, but I knew we needed to do something. So we identified five core values: Faith, Relationships, Vision, Excellence, and Integrity. We wanted these words—and the actions associated with them—to describe our every action. You might point out that the Bible sums up your group's

core values. Yes, but the danger there is that the Bible is so full of truth that without a specific focus you may end up doing none of it. With core values, we were saying that *in our ministry we choose to place value on these five things* (or eight, six, three, in your case). We want to emphasize *these* traits.

How to use core values. Once you have developed your mission statement, you will rally your leaders and your group to that cause and pursue it resolutely. Your core values will dictate how you accomplish your mission, steering you and all the others within your ministry. Core values say, "We value this behavior so much that we will abide by these things, no matter what."

How to create core values. You may wonder how to create core values for your group. I would look to the group itself and discern some of the biggest challenges that you have. Are your kids always putting down one another? Then maybe a core value needs to be, "We will encourage and lift each other up." Adopt this as a core value and have the members of your group sign an agreement to abide by this value. Another challenge might be your teens' disobedience and not respecting leadership. So a core value could be, "We will honor our leaders." If you value honesty, you may create a core value that says, "We will act with integrity." Define the nature and the character of your group through the values you declare important.

Distribute them. Once you've adopted your core values, print and distribute them. Put them on mouse pads, plaques, and shirts. Just like your mission statement, you want these to be at the front of everyone's consciousness.

The real power of core values. The real power begins when you plant these values into the hearts of your students. It will become an attitude. You probably don't even want to call them core values. You could call them something like: the "Five Fighting Points of a World Changer;" or if your group is called Wildfire, "Five Wild Points of

Your core values will dictate how you accomplish your mission.

Planning is the work of a leader; it's your
desk time that makes what is up
front valid and credible.

Wildfire," etc. You are telling students: "This is our code;
this is the way we live; this is our identity."

Core values create corporate culture. Ultimately, after
you have talked about it many times, shown them examples, passed out the cards, and made up the shirts, this men-
tality *will* take hold. You make an agreement that if someone
goes against your core values, anyone can call him or her on
it. You should even give them permission to call you on it,
if they think you're in violation. (I've done just that here at
Teen Mania. Any intern can confront me, or any member of
the staff, if they think we're not living up to the code.)

You must find creative ways to keep these core values
visible. Remind students again and again. What will ulti-

mately happen is this: when you
are not around, your kids will
enforce these values with *each
other*. It will happen *without you
because it has become a part of the
culture.* You won't have to be the
code enforcer because they will
have taken ownership and
grabbed hold of these values for
themselves.

When you get that kind of
pressure working for you, hal-
lelujah! You are on the right path. You won't have to run the
store all the time; the core values will set the atmosphere
and direction of the group.

Start planning today. Planning takes patience and perseverance, and, quite truthfully, it isn't always very exciting. The fruit of planning, however, is awesome! Planning is the work of a leader; it's your desk time that makes what is up front valid and credible.

Read over the notes you made about your dreams for your group so that they are fresh in your mind. Then open the CD-ROM again to the "Why Plan" section and begin to work on your core values.

Pray for God's guidance as you develop these two pillars, your mission statement and core values, for your ministry. Start doing the silent work of a leader.

1. "Sample Mission Statements for Inspiration," Family Business Experts, http://www.family-business-experts.com/sample-mission-statements.html (accessed October 26, 2005).
2. Ibid.
3. Ibid.
4. Ibid.

CHAPTER TWO

BHAGs: Defining Them and Going For It!

There is a cancer in youth ministry that has plagued us for a long time. It's the idea of *feeling holy when you are faithful with a few.* What a tragedy to have the potential within us to do something that affects hundreds (or even thousands) for the Kingdom and not tap into it!

Our "holy, faithful" folks grieve me because everything I see in the Bible tells me this: when God's favor is upon a thing, it grows. If a ministry is alive with His Spirit, it thrives and flourishes. If we haven't figured out how to grow it, maybe it just means we haven't found the right nutrients. Certainly, it doesn't mean the ministry isn't *supposed* to grow.

When God's favor is upon a thing, it grows.
If a ministry is alive with His Spirit, it
thrives and flourishes.

It isn't a pride issue. It's just that God cares about kids —all kids. And when you start reaching a lot of them, they add up.

Some may say, "Well I have tried everything and I still have 10 students in my group, so God must not want me to grow." That person is in danger of *letting his experience dictate his theology, rather than God's Word.* Maybe he has just not tried the right things yet. Therefore, a part of your whole planning process is to attack the attitude that says you can't do it, that you aren't supposed to reach a lot of teens.

Once you've created your mission statement and determined your core values, the next step in the process is to develop some BHAGs, Big Holy Anointed Goals (or, as some like to say, Big Hairy Audacious Goals).

WHAT ARE BHAGS (PRONOUNCED BEEHAGS)?

A study was conducted of successful companies to identify a number of things that these companies had in common. One thing very clearly set them apart from all others: every single one of them had huge goals. They didn't settle for five or ten percent growth in a year. Instead, they set the bar much higher. As they planned and pursued that giant goal, they grew exponentially. What a shame that secular companies can dream more than many leaders in the Body of Christ.

Take NASA, for example. In 1960, John F. Kennedy announced his intention to put a man on the moon by the end of the decade. That goal seemed bigger than life. Not quite impossible, but stunning to think that maybe we could just do it! Money poured in. The nation rallied around its president and its rocket scientists—and the first rocket launched from the pad! Then another and another. Each one took on a bit more adventure, a bit more of the space between Earth and moon. Then, in 1969, Neil Armstrong finally took "one small step for man, one giant leap for mankind." President Kennedy was long buried, but he had given the nation a tangible dream. The nation responded with hard work and success.

BHAGs galvanize the dream. They are a statement of the faith of the leader. BHAGs don't seem possible in the natural, but they don't seem completely off the map either. They may not seem reasonable at first, but they are not irrational in scope. If President Kennedy had said, "Let's put a man on every planet in the solar system," people would not have supported that. But they could grasp the possibility of the moon. Tough to believe, but within the realm of possibility. So, your BHAG could not be "We'll have a million kids in this youth group by the end of the year." Okay, it *could* happen . . . but most people will think it's ludicrous. This doesn't mean, however, that you shouldn't have BHAGs that *seem impossible, but just might be attainable.*

Andy Grove, former CEO of Intel Corporation, had what some people thought was a "crazy" goal. He wanted to double the speed of the computer chip every 18 months. The company has done it, and they keep beating that 18-month time frame.[1] Most big companies like Intel have a

BHAGs don't seem possible in the natural, but they don'tseem completely off the map either.

few huge, looming goals that say: "Just take aim at this!" Those somewhat outrageous goals pull everybody together to focus on getting great things done.

STEP 1: TIME TO DEVELOP YOUR BHAGS

Now is the time to take your dream and put some meat on the bones. It is time to start putting specific goals for the first year of ministry on the table. Where do you want to be in one year? Two years? Three years? Five years? Can you dare to dream as big as God dreams and set some real goals? Can you see your ministry doubling in size in the next 12 months? Can you imagine an amazingly cool youth room? A worship band? Can you imagine doubling again the next year, and again the next? Remember what it says in Ephesians 3:20: "[He] is able to do immeasurably more than all we ask or imagine, according to his power that is at work within us." That means if you can think it, He can do 100 times more than that.

Keep in mind the question we asked during the dreaming process: *If Jesus were the youth leader in my church, what would the group look like in a year? . . . in five years?*

Specifically, how many kids might be here? You dream and then bring that dream into *specific* focus. In other words, a BHAG gives you something concrete to step on as you walk toward your dream. And it is always bigger than what seems possible.

Setting some Big Holy Anointed Goals will crystallize your dream into a very concrete direction. It will show your group and leadership team that you are serious about taking this generation back!

There are three distinct advantages of having BHAGs:

1. BHAGs inspire faith and commitment.
Unfortunately, big goals can often discourage people if

they are not conveyed in the right ways. I used to announce, "I want three thousand kids on the mission field next year." At the time, we had 500. Naturally, my staff members were immediately discouraged, thinking they would be working 24/7 throughout the next year! If we don't introduce our BHAGs properly, they can be a heavy load to others and hardly inspiring.

Let it not be! BHAGs can inspire great faith, virtually *daring* your faithful workers to believe. And this is a good thing. After all, the kids themselves want to be part of something that's bigger than they are, bigger than life. We want them to say, "This is the most happening thing I have ever seen in my life, and I want to commit every spare minute of my time to it!" Why would a kid ever say that? Because he's identified with the mission statement and the BHAGs connected to it!

One thing to know about commitment: one reason a coach often enjoys more commitment than the "youth guy" is that he gives his players BHAGs from day one. "Guys, I really think we could go to state this year. If we do *this* kind of work, do *this* workout, and run plays like *this*, I really think we could do it." And his players, who hope against hope, begin to believe it too.

We must give teens a vision that will capture their attention, their hearts, and their energy—or the world will.

2. BHAGs define the dream.
So you have your dream, and it's sort of "out there." You have all kinds of ideas scratched on paper, and you've refined them with your must-haves (and also a few "nice-to-haves"), but it's still kind of broad. Here's where BHAGs

Now is the time to take your dream and put some meat on the bones.

We must give teens a vision that will capture their attention, their heart, and their energy—or the world will.

help you focus. They put *numbers* to your dream. Yes, you're going to make a big impact . . . but *how* big?

Here is an example:

1. By the end of this year, I would like to have X number of things happening, with X number of kids.
2. By the end of two years, I would like X kids doing these things.
3. By the end of five years, I would like X churches in our town working together on these X projects.

This gives you a way to evaluate your success. It's hard to know if you're doing things right if you only have a vague goal to grow. A BHAG lets you define what you're trying to accomplish, so you can know whether you're accomplishing it or not.

Just like President Kennedy's specific BHAG inspired a nation, an effective BHAG can make the hair stand up on the back of your neck. It inspires and pulls people together to go after your amazing goal.

3. BHAGs force you to take action.

Lots of people find it fairly easy to sit and dream, never putting their names on the line. But is it really better to with-hold your name just so no one will ever know whether you accomplished anything or not? Instead, BHAGs proclaim to the world, "This is what I am signing up for, planning for, and working for. This is where we are going."

They force you to get off the sidelines. You don't have to be pretentious about it. Just roll it out and tell folks that you believe with all your heart that this is the dream God has called you to.

If you make that goal—or 80 percent of it—praise God! Look at how much you have grown. If you shoot for the stars and make it to the moon, you did well. It's better than sitting down and just *looking* at the stars.

For years at Teen Mania we've had awesome BHAGs, and we've typically accomplished them at a level of half or three-quarters of the way. But we made it a lot further than we would have had we settled for no big goals at all (or tiny, safe goals).

STEP 2: WHAT WILL IT TAKE?

Make a master list of everything you'll need. I know this doesn't sound like rocket science, but seriously, sit down and ask yourself, "What is it going to take to pull this off?" Then start writing. Once you have your BHAGs clearly laid out, then start writing down *everything* you'll need to accomplish these goals. Everything. Assume the sky's the limit, and money is no object. Your list might begin with things like . . . money.

(Be careful here. Some "youth guys" assume that if they just get the money then they'll accomplish their BHAGs. It actually takes a lot more than money to do what you want to do. The best approach is to write down everything you need,

An effective BHAG can make the hairstand up on the back of your neck. It inspires and pulls people together to go after your amazing goal.

and then write out next to each item how much it might cost, if money is a factor.)

- *money*
- *a place to meet*
- *adult volunteers*
- *teen leaders*
- *printed materials*
- *media equipment*
- *transportation plans, buses*
- *supplies of all kinds*
  and on . . . and on . . . and on . . .
  (make this a long list!)

You're putting some legs to your vision by asking yourself: What is every single thing I need, whether it's human or physical stuff, in order to get that BHAG accomplished? Now some of these things might seem completely unattainable, but it doesn't matter at this point; just write them down.

Of course, this list is more than a practical planning tool. It's also a big item on your daily prayer list. You have something to bring before the Lord with an aching heart, lifting your specific petitions to Him—because of the kids who must be reached. Will God fail to respond?

And don't forget: you'll find it much easier to get buy-in from others if you have a tangible need list. After all, you're not the only one who must believe in the dream and the BHAGs. You must have many other people with you to do this, right? So as you introduce your BHAGs and speak enthusiastically about them, be sure to have a thorough and specific answer to the question, "What, exactly, do you need to get this to happen?"

I would encourage you to build the list together with a team of your leaders (or people you would like to become your leaders). This way, *you* set the direction as the leader (with agreement from your pastor), but you get others to buy into the dream since they are a part of thinking through what it will take to get there. When you tell your key leaders about your dream and its BHAGs, be careful how you word them. Here is something that works well:

"Let me ask you all something. I have been praying and thinking a lot lately, and I feel that God wants to do something HUGE here in our youth ministry. What if God wants us to grow to 200 by the end of the year and have _____(whatever your BHAGs are). What if this were God's plan? What would it take to get there? What would we need to do to be ready for it?"

> *"What if this is God's plan?"*
> *"Just what if God really wants us to have 500 kids here?"*
> *"I'm not saying I heard directly from God. But what if?"*

Do you see what this little question does? It unlocks their imaginations. "If, just by chance, I actually *have* heard from God, then what do you folks think it would take to get there?" People naturally start brainstorming the possibilities:

"Well, just *if* . . . then we'd need to do *this* and *this* and that."

"Really?" you say. "So you think if we did *that* and *that* and *that*, we could attain this BHAG?"

You're putting some legs to your vision by asking yourself: What is every single thing I need, whether it's human or physical stuff, in order to get that BHAG accomplished?

"Yeah, we do."

"Well, then, what else would we need?"

"Maybe we'd need *this* and *this* and *this* . . ."

See how it goes? People start contributing, and they believe the possibilities. And you already have your list, so you can add your own ideas in the conversational gaps. *You're helping them see the believability* of the BHAG while maintaining an exhaustive laundry list of everything you think it might take. "So you guys are telling me that if we did this and this and this, we could have 500 kids at the end of the year? Hallelujah! Let's start praying over these things."

You're simply being a wise leader. You don't go to them with all the things on your list and try forcing it through because "God told me." Oh, you'll share a few ideas, of course. But let the church leaders and members come up with their own lists so you can add to it as necessary. You're allowing them to participate in the building of this thing so they'll be there with you as it unfolds.

Go to your computer now and open the CD-ROM file titled

"BHAGs," and begin to record some of your big ministry goals in the first section. As you develop those BHAGs (Big Holy Anointed Goals), think about everything it will take to implement those BHAGs and itemize them in the next section. It's very important to spend time with your team praying for these things that will make your ministry successful.

STEP 3: WHAT ARE THE BARRIERS?

You've got the list of what will it take. You've put monetary figures next to each item. Now you pull your team in and talk to them about the opposition.

Write the word BARRIERS at the top of a large sheet of newsprint. Then go for it! You're looking at your BHAGs and you're looking at the list of everything you need; now you write down the things that will try to stop you.

What are the hardest things on your list to acquire? Think long and hard about this together. Try to leave nothing out. Determine to be open, honest, and vulnerable with your team and/or the people working with you. List all the things that are screaming at you, saying, "There's *no* way!"

At first you'll hear only one response: money. Everybody thinks money is the most ferocious BHAG-eating monster. But no, there are a lot of other barriers, and many are much more terrifying than money.

Some more scary barriers: *we need the pastor to buy into youth ministry a lot more.* Or: *we need parents to help us.* And: *we don't even have our own youth facility.*

Write them all down.

Why? So you have something in writing—a "whine list"? No. We write down all the barriers *so we have a target for prayer.*

We can't pretend there are no barriers. We Youth Specialists are like Joshuas heading into the promised land. We know the giants wait there with spears and swords, ready to squash us. But we're going in anyway. We're taking the land by the power of the Lord. But we won't be ignorant about it. We know what wants to stop us, and we plan accordingly.

Make a point of writing down the areas that you can see no possible way to get around. Once you have all the barriers listed you can ask your leaders, "So, if we can find a way through these barriers, we can accomplish these BHAGs?" Then when they give their agreement, it is time to attack!

You can prepare for this meeting with your team by preparing ahead of time. Anticipate some of the barriers they will suggest and record them in "Step Three" of your CD-ROM file "BHAGs." Remember, the purpose of this list is to have a target for prayer!

Lift up those barriers and attack them, one by one. Dealing with barriers is how you unlock ideas. Let's assume you've used a meeting—or several meetings—to list all your barriers. The next time you get together, you'll say, "Let's take this single barrier, right here: transportation. We're going to *attack* this thing! We're going to take one hour and we're not talking about anything but this. Ready?"

Then let the ideas flow—no limits, no hindrances, no boundaries on creativity. You're looking for the one brilliant concept that will (immediately or eventually) make that barrier go away.

It's not exactly brainstorming. You don't say: *What about this? Have we tried that? Oh, that doesn't work.*

No. You attack it. In other words, you take all the reasons that you think you can't beat that thing and you list them all out. And you force onto the table every idea on how to deal with transportation. Get them all out there without judging any of them. We could try this, we could try this, we could try this . . . let the process go to the end. The very end. Go until you've got a big list of possible solutions and don't dismiss a single one.

Now look at all the different possible scenarios and start producing what I call *brain sweat*. You're forcing your brain to attack something that seems impossible to resolve. It will feel as if you're pounding a brick wall and there's no way through. You're pounding and pounding, and forcing your brain to attack instead of saying, "There's no way."

In my experience, something amazing happens then, though it may take several hours, or even several days. At some point, someone will suddenly say, *"You know what? If we did this . . ."* and—eureka! The solution suddenly emerges! I can't tell you how many times we've been in the middle of our planning meetings, and in the midst of a brutal attack on a barrier—when we're all becoming fatigued and frustrated—there it is. The breakthrough.

It's been a puzzle, and the pieces suddenly fit together. And maybe it doesn't take any money after all!

Most often, you don't need money as much as you need *ideas* from people who know how to work the creative minds God has given them. (Of course, if you really do need money, gather those folks to you. Who better to help you crash that barrier?)

Breakthrough ideas. These are what you are hunting for. One golden idea could be worth a million souls or a

Dealing with barriers is how you unlock ideas.

One golden idea could be worth a million souls or a million dollars.

million dollars. People think they need dollars, but they are wrong. They need ideas from heaven that will inspire people and change lives!

Breakthrough ideas unlock solutions. Wow. Those are the ideas that carry you through from dreams to action, traversing all the steps in between.

Not every idea is a golden idea, but when you get one, it could mean a lot of fruit for the kingdom of God. The key is to attack barriers *one by one*. You can't hit them all at once. But if you prioritize and clear away the ones that have annoyed you the longest, you'll have some breakthrough ideas staring you in the face as a result.

Yes, it's hard work. You've got to wrestle and you've got to sweat. But in the end, through the *people* God gives you, God will give you the *ideas*, too.

WHO'S THE REAL COMPETITION?

As you think through your BHAGs, here's a wonderful and quite relevant passage of Scripture to keep in mind:

> *Jesus and his disciples went out into the Judean countryside, where he spent some time with them, and baptized. Now John also was baptizing at Aenon near Salim, because there was plenty of water, and people were constantly coming to be baptized. (This was before John was put in prison.) An argument developed between some of John's disciples and a certain Jew over the matter of ceremonial washing. They came to John and said to him, "Rabbi, that man who was with you on the other side of*

the Jordan—the one you testified about—well, he is bap-
tizing, and everyone is going to him."

To this John replied, "A man can receive only what
is given him from heaven. You yourselves can testify
that I said, 'I am not the Christ but am sent ahead of
him.' The bride belongs to the bridegroom. The friend
who attends the bridegroom waits and listens for him,
and is full of joy when he hears the bridegroom's voice.
That joy is mine, and it is now complete. He must
become greater; I must become less."

—John 3:22–30

John's disciples had a strange complaint: "Jesus is bap-
tizing and gaining more followers than you are, John!" Did
John take up a competitive spirit? (This happens all the time
in youth ministry.)

As you develop your BHAGs, keep reminding yourself
that it's not about having a *bigger* group than the guy down
the street or in the next city. It's about beating our real competition, the devil and all of the millions he's trying to pull
into his kingdom with MTV, Hollywood, and Grand Theft
Auto video games. That is who our enemy is. It's definitely
not each other.

John the Baptist says a person can only have what is
given to him from heaven. So why should we try to compare our gifts and our callings and our ministries to others?
On the contrary, we can glean all kinds of great ideas from
other youth ministries who are faithfully following God's
will. And we can offer to help those around us.

Then, when someone comes to you as they did with
John—and they tell you that Joe Youth Pastor has a *much*
bigger group—you can praise God for His goodness and
grace in Joe's life. You can refuse to let a competitive spirit
hurt your own ministry. All of us together are attending the
wedding, but Jesus alone is the Bridegroom.

Develop your BHAGs, figure out what they'll need, and attack your obstacles. Don't worry about what others are doing, or how much. This is God's call on your life. Live His specific vision for you.

1. Brent Schlender "How Intel Took Moore's Law from Idea to Ideology," *Fortune*, November 11, 2002.

CHAPTER THREE

Organizing and Managing the Plan

You have your mission statement, your core values, and your BHAGs. You're forming a team, and you're building planning time into your schedule. Now let's move on to the next step in turning your dreams into reality.

"That's a lot to do!" you shout, "Where do I find the time?" Obviously this all takes time. If you will actually implement the very practical, hands-on, proven steps I suggest in each chapter, you will impact many teens in your region. Not only that, you will save yourself much time and energy in the process. Trust me on this: the results will be worth it! You will see how in this chapter.

How do I stay on top of the present in order to find time to plan for the future?

In my ministry, as I learned how to work planning into my schedule, I recognized that there are two categories of time: (1) time to manage the *Now Plan* (for maintenance), and (2) time to invent the *Future* (for growth). This chapter will deal with organizing and managing the plan you have developed so far, and the next chapter will deal with inventing the Future.

Understanding and using these two modes of time will help the Youth Specialist plan for the future and avoid burnout. National statistics show that youth workers are resigning from churches on an average of every 18–21 months.[1] Clearly, we all need to develop a rhythm in our lives that refreshes us and carries us along in faith, productivity, and peace. That way, we can keep pursuing our dreams. Our BHAGs won't burn us out; they'll fuel us.

The *Now Plan* helps us do this through a kind of compacting process. That is, it helps us take everything we're doing right now and compress it into a smaller part of our time, so we have more time to plan for the future. At Teen Mania, we call the *Now Plan* "Friday's Payroll." It's everything that must happen to keep the wheels turning and the ministry going.

ORGANIZING THE NOW PLAN, STEP BY STEP

As we wrestle with ever-increasing demands on our time, the question on all our minds is, *how do I stay on top of the present in order to find time to plan for the future?* Let's look at the answer in six steps:

1. Determine what's absolutely critical. As you look at your BHAGs for the next 12 months, ask yourself, *What are the five or six areas absolutely critical to your success?* Carefully think this through: "For me to even have a shot at accomplishing this BHAG, what *must* succeed?" Or put it like this: "These six things must not fail . . ."

We call these Critical Success Factors. They are the things that absolutely must happen, no matter what. Everything else can fail, but these *cannot* fail because everything else is built upon them.

Often, our problem is that we spend a lot of time and energy ensuring the success of many things—but they aren't the critical things! The remedy is to realize that some of the things taking your time must be pruned away. We hang on to too many ministry obligations out of tradition. If a certain activity has nothing to do with your mission statement or your BHAGs, it is time to let it go.

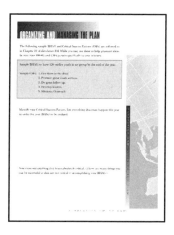

How do you decide what is critical? Can you read it in a book? Consult with a genius? Choosing the Critical Success Factors is the task of the leader— *you* must choose. You can ask others or read books to gain insight, but every ministry and vision is different and ultimately *you* have to make the decision. Remember, you do have the Holy Spirit to help you; you're not alone!

At Teen Mania we use a process of identifying those elements that are vital to the success of our ministry and monitoring them to be sure we stay on course. Go to your computer now and open the CD-ROM file "Organizing." This page details the planning process we use to list and track these Critical Success Factors.

Let's talk in practical terms now. Let's say your BHAG is to have 120 on-fire teens in your group by the end of the year. You have 10 kids now, and you want 12 times that number by the end of the year. Therefore, a factor crucial to your success will be to get more people to come. I know that sounds pretty simple, but if everything is great week after week, but no one comes through your doors to see it, then you will never reach your BHAG. You have to find a way to get people through the door. This, then, is your Critical Success Factor #1: *Get them in the door.* It's critical, so write it down.

At this point, you have only one factor to focus on, not 95, so you can probably handle a couple more. Let's say you have 40 new kids coming each week but they're not committing their lives to Christ. They are all bored, and during your sermon they pass notes instead of taking notes. Yes, they are coming in the door, but you're not engaging them in the things of God once they are there. How can you capture their hearts for God when they come to your meetings? You do that by having amazing youth services. Put that down—Critical Success Factor #2: *Produce great youth services.*

Now you have a great youth service, and you have people getting saved. But nobody is following up with your teens. No one is helping them get strong. Kids are coming in, getting rocked, and then heading right out the back door. So you must write that down as critical to achieve your BHAG—Critical Success Factor #3: *Do great follow-up.*

Your Critical Success Factors may be different than these. But whatever they are, they'll focus you. They'll make you chop your calendar to pieces and cut out the useless wheel-spinning that's unrelated to the mission. Monitoring these three factors will eventually make you admit: "There is too much work for me to do by myself. I must develop others around me to take responsibility." Write it down! Critical Success Factor #4: *Develop leaders who can take responsibility.*

Let's stop here and open Resource #1 on your CD-ROM. As you can see, this page helps to identify factors critical to the success of one of your BHAGs. It is the work of the leader to figure out these factors and weigh the importance of each one. Write the first BHAG you want to work on in the space provided, and list its Critical Success Factors below it.

2. Turn your Critical Success Factors into your job description. Let's assume you have listed five Critical Success Factors for your first BHAG. These five areas now become your *job description.* Summarize them into one statement and record it on this page. This, and only this, is the specific work you will spend your time doing as a youth pastor. Duplicate this page and follow the same process for each of your other BHAGs. The results of this think-time will be the foundation for your successful youth ministry!

Now that you have identified the Critical Success Factors for each of your BHAGs for the year, determine concrete, measurable goals for each factor, broken down by week and month. Why measurable? *What you measure is what actually gets done.*

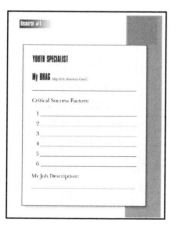

Now open Resource 2 on your CD-ROM and look at the illustration called "Getting to My BHAG." This is a helpful goal-setting tool. I will use the example from earlier in the chapter. My BHAG is: *"I want to have 120 on-fire teens in my group by the end* of the year." The first Critical Success Factor is: *"Get them in the door."* What are the concrete, measurable goals to accomplish this?

To begin with, I must ask myself: "How many people

do I need to get in the door, and what percentage need to get saved and stay in order to end up with 120?"

Let's break it down to make it easier: "If I have 40 kids visit every month, then 12 times 40 is 480 kids visiting by the end of the year. Forty visitors per month is 10 per week. *Notice that I've written "10" in my weekly goal box.*

Now out of 480 kids who visit, could I lead half of them to Christ? Yes, I think so. That would be 240 new believers, or five per week. *I've written "5" as my weekly goal.*

If I have 240 new believers, could I get half of them discipled? I think I could. I indicated each of these figures on the chart. Recording these smaller, concrete goals will help me track my progress toward achieving my big BHAG.

Now it's your turn. Go to the next screen on your CD-ROM and look at the blank page, "Getting to My BHAG." Begin by writing the BHAG you wish to work on in the space provided. Then name the first Critical Success Factor on the line below it. Continue by listing the smaller, measurable targets that you must accomplish each week and month in order to successfully hit the year-end goal. A tally of these boxes will give you a monthly target to shoot for.

During the month, you will constantly monitor your progress compared to your written goals. Maybe this month you are doing great on numbers one and two but are falling behind with number three. *Then that is where you need to spend your time.* Repeat this process for each Critical Success Factor related to this BHAG. You can reproduce this page and line them up side by side on a table or tape them to the wall. (Several extra blank charts are available to you in this part of the CD-ROM.) This will give you an instant overview of the year, as pictured in the last page of Resource #2. You will see at a glance whether or not you are on track to meet the BHAG.

This chart includes a sample BHAG and Critical Success Factors (CSFs). You will incorporate your own BHAG and CSFs when charting your plan on the CD-ROM.

Getting to My BHAG

The following chart breaks down the Critical Success Factors used by Ron Luce and Teen Mania in a week-by-week format.

BHAG: *To have 120 on-fire teens in my group by the end of the year.*

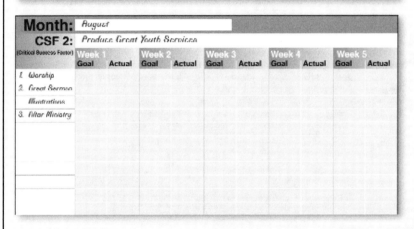

Month:	August									

CSF 1: Get Them In the Door

(Critical Success Factor)

	Week 1		Week 2		Week 3		Week 4		Week 5	
	Goal	Actual	Goal	Actual	Goal	Actual	Goal	Actual	Goal	Actual
1. Visitors	10		10		10		10			
2. Salvations	5		5		5		5			
3. Discipled	2		3		2		3			

Use these boxes to break down your Critical Success Factors into smaller measurable goals.

Month:	August									

CSF 2: Produce Great Youth Services

(Critical Success Factor)

	Week 1		Week 2		Week 3		Week 4		Week 5	
	Goal	Actual	Goal	Actual	Goal	Actual	Goal	Actual	Goal	Actual
1. Worship										
2. Great Sermon Illustrations										
3. Altar Ministry										

Depending on your BHAG, there are several other areas to think about that may be critical to your success:

- *developing teen leaders*
- *adult volunteers*
- *worship team (to create dynamic services)*
- *drama team (to help with great services)*

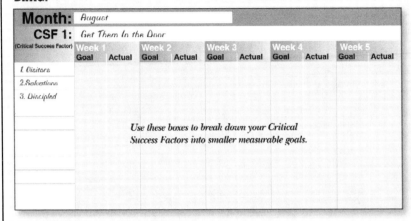

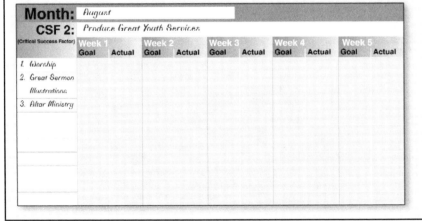

The following images contain the resource chart:

Resource #2

Getting to My BHAG

The following chart breaks down the Critical Success Factors used by Ron Luce and Teen Mania in a week-by-week format.

BHAG: To have 120 on-fire teens in my group by the end of the year.

Month: August

CSF 1: (Critical Success Factor) Get Them In the Door

	Week 1 Goal	Actual	Week 2 Goal	Actual	Week 3 Goal	Actual	Week 4 Goal	Actual	Week 5 Goal	Actual
1. Visitors										
2. Salvations										
3. Discipled										

Use these boxes to break down your Critical Success Factors into smaller measurable goals.

Month: August

CSF 2: (Critical Success Factor) Produce Great Youth Services

	Week 1 Goal	Actual	Week 2 Goal	Actual	Week 3 Goal	Actual	Week 4 Goal	Actual	Week 5 Goal	Actual
1. Worship										
2. Great Sermon Illustrations										
3. Altar Ministry										

- missions recruitment (to make changing the world a norm)
- sermon topics

It is important to remember—especially when considering sermon topics—that some of your BHAGs should have to do with *what qualities you're trying to invest in your students.* If you want kids with servants' hearts, kids who love to worship, and kids who reach out to others, then that will dictate what you preach about. You will spend a month emphasizing giving, or missions, or exploring and meeting the needs of people around you.

One advantage to carefully planning and charting your BHAGs is that you will be continually thinking in terms of the big picture and long-term goals for your group. As you see stories and statistics, object lessons and video clips, you'll be splicing them into your ministry plans. "Oh, that will fit in with October's sermons! I'll save it in my file so it will be there for me when I need it." Every sermon you do, every nugget you offer, from this point on, should be directly related to your mission statement and to your BHAGs.

3. Use a flowchart to structure your ministry. A flow-chart visually lays out how the dream will come to pass. It puts structure to your dream. You are building an organization (even if it's with all volunteers) to accomplish the

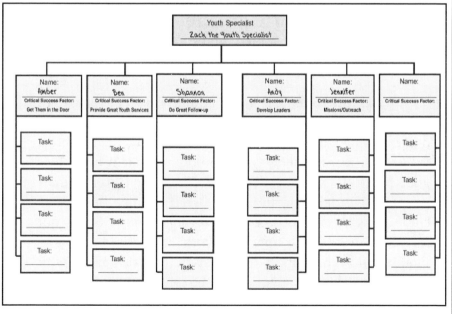

Your staff, whether volunteer or paid, needs to immediately see that they are functioning in a dynamic environment of great possibilities for multiplying growth.

dream. You are enlisting others' energy to accomplish the vision that God has given you.

Take some time now to examine the sample flowchart in Resource #3 of the CD-ROM. The row of boxes at the top of the page should directly correlate to your list of Critical Success Factors. If you have five Critical Success Factors, you will fill out five columns, each labeled with the name of one of the factors. (Ultimately, you should have an adult volunteer in charge of each one of your Critical Success Factors so you are not doing it all by yourself. We'll discuss that more in the next section.)

4. Recruit teens and adult volunteers to be "staff" in your ministry. All the blank names in each of the top boxes must be filled by a qualified adult "leader" of that area. When you recruit them, you should show them how their goals relate to the overall BHAGs. You have some smart people in your church, and they'll want to know that if they come and give their time *it will be highly leveraged.* So lay out for them in advance how the work is distributed. Show them the flowchart and where they fit. (We deal more with recruiting and training your dream team in future chapters.)

Help them understand how they fit into the mission statement and your specific one-year goals related to the BHAG. Don't just say, "Here, go to work, bring in visitors." Instead you'll say, "I want you to understand the big picture. While you are working on bringing in the visitors, we have other people working on the services, and others on outreach." Your staff, whether volunteer or paid, needs to immediately see that they are functioning in a dynamic environment of great possibilities for multiplying growth.

Naturally, they won't do the job exactly as you might do it. They might do it only 80 percent as well as you could. That's okay! *If you have five people working at 60 percent, that is 300 percent more manpower than what you have by yourself.*

5. Work with your staff to develop their Critical Success Factors. You need to take charge of the factors critical to the success of your big goals; so do the people on your staff. As leader, your job is to show your staff how to do this. Suppose, for example, you have someone responsible for Outreach. Her job is to get 40 people to attend meetings every month. So print out a blank copy of the Youth Staff Member form, (Resource #4 of the CD-ROM) give it to her and ask, "What are the top four things you need to do in order to get 40 kids here each month?"

"Well, I need to have some brochures. I need to have somebody inviting them. I need . . ." Whatever those things are, help her get those things. Do this planning *with* her by charting each of her Critical Success Factors.

Now create a flowchart for her, just like the one you have. Note that *her chart of Critical Success Factors falls organizationally under a single Critical Success Factor of yours.*

You are multiplying your ministry!

Help her break the task down still further. Each of her critical success areas must have a volunteer (teen or adult) overseeing that area. This gives all of your teens in your group a place to plug into the vision.

6. *Set up a regular reporting process.* By working with each of your "leadership team" members to set the critical success factors for their areas, you now have the structure for a weekly report. You want to keep your finger on the "ministry pulse" week by week, month by month. Don't wait until the end of the year to ask, "How are you doing with your Critical Success Factors?" Instead, tell your helpers, "I want to hear from you on a regular basis, maybe every week or every other week. I want to know how things are going, so I can be ready to help you out, if you need it."

Then if goals aren't met, you can walk through the charts with that person and his team. "Let's look at the five things you needed to do, and let's figure out which of these things did not really work." Your job as a leader becomes coaching, encouraging, and brainstorming with your leaders. Don't ever just ask, "Why didn't you do that?" No, *you* are there to help them figure it out creatively.

You can check the incremental movements toward goals by looking at the Critical Success Factor tasks that are completed or not completed. For example, if your goal is to get 40 visitors per month, and you're only getting 30, go talk with that leader. Maybe one of her CSFs was to print a thousand flyers a month and pass them out. You can ask, "Did you actually print a thousand flyers?"

You might hear: "No, I only printed 500." That could be why people aren't coming—they don't know about the meetings. Talk about it. Adjust.

Or maybe she answers: "We had them printed, but they weren't distributed." Okay, then what needs to change so that the distribution takes place? Talk about it. Brainstorm.

With this kind of process, people can see which part of their plan is failing. They can pick up on trends and take proactive actions. Receiving regular reports from your staff will help you monitor progress and the overall ministry trends. Adjust accordingly.

Are you starting to see the picture here? You can accomplish much more by enlisting others in the dream and showing them how their role helps to accomplish the BHAG. In doing this you have just redefined your job description. Instead of running around like a chicken with your head cut off, you have a team of people each doing his or her part of the vision. You have multiplied yourself and are saving a lot of time and wear and tear on your body (as well as on your family!).

So, that is how you organize and manage the *Now Plan*. It will help you define where you need to spend your time. You will cut down on busywork activities and focus your energy on the things that count—the factors critical to the success of your BHAGs. The people who work with you will put their time into their areas of critical success. As a result, you can chart your progress and *multiply your ministry!* I think a miracle is about to happen in your youth group!

1. "Our Passion," Youth Link Ministries, http://www.youthlinkministries.com/ (accessed October 25, 2005).

CHAPTER FOUR

Inventing the Future

We've gone deeply into the mechanics of the *Now Plan* in the previous chapter. But what about planning for the future? You have to do more than maintenance to win a generation. Here at Teen Mania, we call it "Inventing the Future." Hopefully, because of the way you're now organized, you will have time in your schedule to regularly *Invent the Future*. If not, you must make time. A big part of the leader's job is to develop the plan for the future. No one else

You have to do more than maintenance to win a generation.

You will not do large things to impact large masses of teens without extensive future planning.

will be thinking about it more than you, so if you don't, they won't.

Here at Teen Mania everyone on staff has two jobs— one is to manage a *Now Plan* for "Friday's payroll," the other is to *Invent the Future*. A staff person's job is not to just keep things going. The other part is for him or her to spend significant time figuring out how to get where we really want to go. The higher you are in the organization, the more time you spend *Inventing the Future*. Remember, the larger you want your ministry to become, the more you have to spend time doing future planning. *You will not do large things to impact large masses of teens without extensive future planning.*

MAKE INVENTING THE FUTURE A REGULAR PRIORITY!

Here's a scene snapshot from the Gospel of John: *"Jesus and His disciples went out into the Judean countryside, **where He spent some time with them**, and baptized"* (John 3:22) (emphasis added).

Now isn't this interesting? In the middle of Jesus' busy life and ministry, He pulls His disciples aside to spend time with them. Together, they withdraw to a lake while a large crowd follows them.

We see this "withdrawing-with-disciples" strategy again and again in the Gospels. Jesus' model of pulling His dedicated followers aside drives home an important point for us today: *We must deliberately set aside time in our lives to plan together for the future, or we will never do anything huge.* I invite you to take note of some basic guidelines when spending time with "your people," as Jesus did.

Spend time away with your leaders to talk about the big plan. Make it a priority to get away with your leaders and adult volunteers to think about one thing and only one thing: *The Big Plan.* Just that, and nothing else. If Jesus could take time out of His busy schedule to do it, certainly you can.

At Teen Mania we take one or two days per month for the leadership team to spend the whole day together. The only thing that we talk about on that day is . . . *the future.* It doesn't matter that there are fires to put out or that the walls are about to crash down around us in our practical, day-to-day problems. On that day, we don't care. We talk only about the future. Sometimes we'll meet here on our campus and other times we'll meet at a lodge or retreat center and make it a long weekend.

At these *Inventing the Future* meetings, we don't talk about our plan of action for the next 12 months—that's discussed at our regular weekly meetings. When we invent the future, we talk about *more than one year* down the road, maybe even three or five years from now. Our agenda will have to do with huge BHAGs that we haven't tackled within this year's plan. For example, we started planning for the Silverdome three years before the actual event. We were inventing the future far in advance. Only after talking about it and researching for a year and a half did we

Make it a priority to get away with your leaders and adult volunteers to think about one thing and only one thing: The Big Plan.

actually announce our plans to the world and invite teens from all over the nation for a weekend stadium event.

Make the agenda crystal clear. So what do we do on those days? We come in with a clear agenda, ready to work. I give everyone an agenda in advance and tell them to bring ideas to the table about a specific topic. This is the work of a leader. We, as leaders, have to tell our people, "I am pulling from your brain the creative ideas that we need in order to plan well. I want you to come ready." Then the team will bring ideas to the table, backed by all the research for those ideas, so that *they present well-thought-through opinions.*

This is key. We don't want our inventing-the-future plan to get sidetracked by random opinions and off-the-cuff notions. We want some meat on those bones! "Tell me *why* you think we should do that." Let your idea-givers also provide the backup, the research, and the thought processes behind the opinion—and then trust their opinion when it is shown to be worthy.

Always give homework assignments. As you dream and think outside the box, ask your staff/volunteers to help gather information needed to move your goals forward: "Between our once-a-month meetings, everyone has a homework assignment! I need to know . . ." If you are thinking about holding a fall youth rally, one person might research which other youth ministries have done big events in September, what kinds of things drew kids, and how many kids came. If you need a band, someone else can research what bands may be available. Maybe you need an auditorium in your town. Assign someone to research what facilities are available.

At the next meeting, you will come back and ask, "What have you learned during this research time?" When everyone brings their items to the table, you can put it all together, think and talk through it, and let it spark new ideas. Then, you can begin to dream outside the box again.

Ideally, you don't want to waste time. This way of approaching the future is to share the work in order to multiply your efforts. In addition, peer pressure is a healthy motivator for everyone to complete assignments. No one wants to be the slacker who leaves things to the last minute or comes unprepared!

Once you've assimilated all the information, you can also identify holes in your data and see what information is still missing. What new questions does the research raise? When you leave that meeting, hand out new assignments for next month, so that when you reconvene you will be that much closer to seeing the BHAG become a reality. Essentially, you're still asking, in many different ways, the planning question we used earlier: "What will it take to accomplish this dream?"

Operate within the fiscal year. We operate according to our fiscal year, which is based on the school year. I think that most youth ministries should, since so much of what we all do revolves around and begins with the school year. When we start our new year in September, we have already been thinking about that year for at least 12 months, discussing it each month in order to be ready. As we implement the plan for the new year, we also start the planning process for the next year. Let me give you a peek at the itinerary of each monthly *Inventing the Future* meeting:

- *September–December*
  We dream way outside the box for the next three to five years.
- *January–March*
  We back up and say, "Well, if we are going to be there in three years, what will we need to do starting this September? Where do we need to be at the end of this year? For this year, what

will our BHAG need to be to achieve the
three-year goal?"

- *April–June*
We plan meticulously what each department will
have to do month by month to accomplish the
next year's goals.

- *July–August*
We do the final preparations to launch the new
year in September that we have been working on
steadily for the past 12 months.

We look at each month, understanding where we need
to be in the planning process so that, by the time April and
May roll around, we have a very clear picture of what that
September will look like—and what the whole coming year
will look like.

We are normally looking three to five years ahead,
asking: Where could we *be* then? What does *that* picture
look like? What could really be happening *then*?

THREE STAGES OF PLANNING

As you think about *Inventing the Future*, you'll have
three steps of planning.

1. The Strategic Plan. Simply put, the Strategic Plan
answers the question, "What strategies are you going to
implement to achieve your BHAG?" In other words, if part
of your BHAG is to draw 100 or 200 visitors each week,
what strategy will you employ to get them there? There are
many strategies that could work. You could do a big event
with a band. You could do a contest with teens, like the
"Great Commission Competition." (See Appendix.) You
could make young people themselves the evangelizers.
With any part of your BHAG there will be a number of
methods to accomplish the goal. How do you choose which
strategy you will use?

Obviously, you can look at what other people have done successfully. Don't, however, fall into the trap of thinking that if you do what someone else does, you will automatically be successful too. You have a unique community, unique visions, and unique teens. So these ideas may work or they may not. How can you tell? Glad you asked!

You can run tests. Running tests is how you can prevent a scenario like this from playing out . . .

"Well, I really feel in my heart that we need to have an event. If we do this and this and this, I know we can get 500 kids there. I just know it!"

So you spend wads of money, bring in a band, and do all kinds of things that you just know will work. And you get 100 kids there. Out of the 100 kids who show up, most are already saved, but three get saved. Then you say . . .

"Oh, I know we still owe the church $1,500 because we lost money on this event, but I don't know where we're going to get that money. I guess we'll have to work for the next year to pay the church back. But if it was for the sake of even one soul it would still have been worth it."

Foolishly, we justify a lot of things we do for that proverbial "one soul," don't we? Yes, every soul is important, but that's not an excuse for us to be bad stewards of our time and resources. Testing an idea before it is implemented will help you be a good steward.

All successful enterprises test their potential ideas. They try a new burger or sandwich in various cities, run the ads, track the sales, and find out whether anyone will buy it before they commit big bucks to it. If it fails, then that particular product won't be added to the menu.

You can test an idea by testing each of its aspects or assumptions.

But how can we do this type of testing in our ministries? Let me suggest that you can test an idea ("I want to do an event where a lot of seeking kids are going to come and hear the Gospel") by *testing each of its aspects or assumptions.*

In the example above, you might first test the band. Run the band's name and its style of music by many of your teens and others in the local high school. If most of your potential market says, "Yeah, that was really great for . . . the '80s!" then you probably won't want those guys to come play for you. It's no fun working hard only to find out later that "no one around here even likes the band"—you were the only one excited. So you do a test, take a poll, or start a focus group to find out what your potential market thinks.

Second, you might test your ideas about "how we'll get kids to attend." We do a lot of "testing" at Teen Mania. For example, maybe you're thinking, "If I put posters everywhere, call every kid in town, and run advertisements on the radio, then that will bring a thousand kids to our event." So you put posters all over South Mall, which *sounded like* a good idea—but none of the kids hang out there. You didn't know that. You got 20 kids from your youth group to make 30 calls per day for x-number of days, but in the end those kids decided not to come.

Instead of calling 1,000 kids for your big event, what if you tested like this: "Let's try a 'medium' event on a regular Wednesday night and let's call 100 kids. We'll get some kids to make the calls, give them an exact script and see—out of those 100—what percentage actually shows up."

You might find that 50 weren't even home, 20 of them hung up on the caller, 10 of them said maybe, another 10 said, "on a cold day in hell would I come," and 10 said they were excited and would, indeed, show up. Seven actually showed up at the event.

Now you have some data you can use to predict results. You know you called 100 kids, and seven showed up. Part of your learning would be that for every 100 calls you make, seven will show up. So if you want 100 teens, how many calls would you need to make? You do the math. That's why you run a test: to see if that effort will actually work and how much of it you'll need to apply to get the results you want. Conclusion? Don't expend all the energy and all the money on the wrong strategy.

Here's another example. Suppose you think it would be just great to run ads on the radio, so you go to the church board and ask for $3,000 to run the ads. After you've run hours of ads you find out that none of the kids listen to that radio station. You seemingly did everything right, but you end up with a lame turnout as a result. Could you have tested the idea first? Could you have asked around to make sure which radio station the teens listen to? Sure!

Ongoing tests help you put together a strategic plan that you can have confidence in. By the time you execute your plan, you can be pretty confident—at least 80 percent sure—that the efforts you're exerting are going to work and actually produce the result you envisioned. You can roll out your plan to everybody—detailing the destination—and have great confidence that you will really arrive. You tested the ideas enough to know that if you do this and this, you will probably get *this* result.

Remember, in life we don't get graded on our intentions; we get graded on our results. We don't even get graded on our efforts toward what failed. Therefore it makes sense, doesn't it, to find out through a testing process whether a plan will likely work?

"But Ron, how can you be so mean?" I hear you say. "People are *really* trying here, spending a ton of time and energy. Can't you give them some credit?"

My response: "Is it really mean to want people to be productive with their lives?" Think about how Jesus put it:

> *"Again, it will be like a man going on a journey, who called his servants and entrusted his property to them.*

Ongoing tests help you put together a strategic plan that you can have confidence in.

To one he gave five talents of money, to another two talents, and to another one talent, each according to his ability. Then he went on his journey. The man who had received the five talents went at once and put his money to work and gained five more. So also, the one with the two talents gained two more. But the man who had received the one talent went off, dug a hole in the ground and hid his master's money.

"After a long time the master of those servants returned and settled accounts with them. The man who had received the five talents brought the other five. 'Master,' he said, 'you entrusted me with five talents. See, I have gained five more.'

"His master replied, 'Well done, good and faithful servant! You have been faithful with a few things; I will put you in charge of many things. Come and share your master's happiness!'

"The man with the two talents also came. 'Master,' he said, 'you entrusted me with two talents; see, I have gained two more.'

"His master replied, 'Well done, good and faithful servant! You have been faithful with a few things; I will put you in charge of many things. Come and share your master's happiness!'

"Then the man who had received the one talent came. 'Master,' he said, 'I knew that you are a hard man, harvesting where you have not sown and gathering where you have not scattered seed. So I was afraid and

went out and hid your talent in the ground. See, here is what belongs to you.'

"His master replied, 'You wicked, lazy servant! So you knew that I harvest where I have not sown and gather where I have not scattered seed? Well then, you should have put my money on deposit with the bankers, so that when I returned I would have received it back with interest.

"'Take the talent from him and give it to the one who has the ten talents. For everyone who has will be given more, and he will have an abundance. Whoever does not have, even what he has will be taken from him. And throw that worthless servant outside, into the darkness, where there will be weeping and gnashing of teeth.'"

—Matthew 25:14–30

This is important stuff from our Lord! It's life or death for His servants. Don't forget about the man who was given the one talent and buried it. Scripture calls him a wicked and lazy servant. You see, the Boss (for us, that's Jesus) expects His servants to be productive. Why? Not because He's mean. It's because deep in His heart He's saying: "I love you and want you to do something productive with your life."

Jesus doesn't want any of us putting out massive efforts that don't pay off. Our job as leaders in the strategic planning process is to ask our staff people, "Have you actually *tried* this and this and this? If not, how do you *know* it will work?" That's a lot different than talking about what they feel will work.

At this point, fill out the CD-ROM file titled "Strategy."

This will give you a chance to strategize the best ways to go about accomplishing your BHAG.

2. The Operational Plan. Look at the flowchart in Resource #3 again. This is a simple device that graphically displays how you will accomplish your operational plan day by day. It ties people and resources to your strategies and specifies *when* and *how* they will come into play throughout the year. What are the critical success factors for

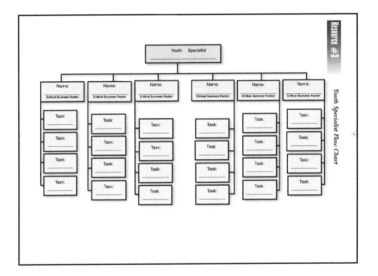

each area? Are you still on target to achieve those goals each week? The flowchart tracks these critical operations for you.

You don't have to be a genius to develop this kind of operational plan, but you do have to sit down and chart things out. To be the most effective, you'll need to be sure that everyone is aware of the accountability tied to his or her specific tasks (which means you'll also need a process of "checking in"—which means regular, updated progress reports). Make the chart accessible to all.

Your operational flowchart takes all the goals and strategies that you know are going to work and divides

Remember: As you do this "unglamorous" work of planning, you will achieve more ministry impact than you ever thought possible.

them into "buckets of responsibility"—who will do what, and when. It figures out what this "execution machine" has to look like if it is to make your strategic goals actually happen. This is the operational plan. Once you plug in your volunteers and all the other resources, you can probably hit your strategic goals.

3. The Financial Plan. This is the subject we all hate to talk about. Money. But it's time to attach dollars to all those initiatives you have been planning, and put a budget together. How much do you have in the revenue stream? Not much? Don't worry and don't be discouraged! Do be realistic.

Sometimes we would love to accomplish a certain strategic plan—we can see how well it would work—but it is just going to cost too much. We can't afford that many staff, or that many brochures. So we crunch the numbers a little more and figure out what we must spend and what we think we could get donated by someone else. We go back and change the operational plan a little—this might work with fewer staff, more volunteers. Or we just try to do something a little smarter.

It's a back and forth process when you work with the finances. Try to creatively balance the operational and financial plans.

Inventing the Future must be a regular priority from now on if you are to continue to pursue the dreams God has for you and your youth ministry. When you make time for it, all your volunteer staff will make it a priority as well. Remember that as you do this "unglamorous" work of planning, you will achieve more ministry impact than you ever thought possible.

The lives you touch will make it worthwhile.

CHAPTER FIVE

Funding Your Plan

"If I just had more money I could . . ." How many times have we said or thought those words? Too often the youth ministry budget is the bottom entry of the church budget—if it's on there at all.

Most of the plans you have developed will take some serious cash to get off the ground. Don't just sit there paralyzed because you think you'll never get that kind of money; if this is God's dream, He will provide. Still, that doesn't mean you should sit around waiting for provision to fall from heaven. There are many things you can do to prepare to receive the blessing of the Lord.

All youth pastors have become experts at fundraisers

> Don't just sit there paralyzed because you think you'll never get that kind of money; if this is God's dream, He will provide.

like car washes and bake sales. I am not going to talk about any of that here—there are many more creative, fresh ways to gather resources for your youth ministry. It costs money to reach teens. It makes me so mad that the world spends billions to reach kids through rock 'n' roll and television, while most youth ministries are on a shoestring budget and can't even afford new curriculum.

Once my daughter Charity was in the kitchen with my wife, Katie. Charity was singing, "If you're happy, and you know it . . . " and Katie was doing the motions. "If you're happy, and you know it, stomp your feet." Several verses later, Charity wanted to see how far she could push it, and sang, "If you're happy, and you know it, give me a dollar." Katie stopped doing the motions.

Too many of our youth fundraisers are the equivalent of this song. We do a lot of activity, make a lot of noise, and end up with little to show for it.

Let me give you some practical steps to getting resources.

THE DREAM COMES BEFORE THE MONEY

Some people think, "If I only had money, then I could dream something great for God." In reality, if you had the money before you had a clear dream from God, you would waste it! Your lack of money isn't what's holding you back; your lack of a dream is. If you will do the planning work of a leader that we've talked about, the money will follow.

How does God lead you? First, He gives you the *vision*,

then He gives you the *PRO-vision*. The first step is having the dream.

Think of the example set by Mary in the Bible. When the angel told her she would give birth to the Son of God, she responded with instant acceptance. She didn't say, "Lord, I'm unmarried and have no means of financial support if I have a baby out of wedlock." After she gave birth, the wise men came from the East with gold, frankincense, and myrrh—gifts which would support Mary and Joseph.

The gifts come after you've committed yourself to God's dream. God's provision *will* come. And it will surprise you. It may be countries and months away, but it *will* come into your life when you need it. Don't wait for the camels to get there before you agree to His dream.

Think about it. What ministry have you ever known that started because they had a ton of money and didn't know what to do with it all? It almost never happens that way. Many people believe that if they worked at a megachurch the pastor would give them a lot of money and they would have a big youth group.

Let me set you free from that myth. First of all, those youth pastors at the big megachurches don't necessarily get big budgets. Let me give you a rule of thumb: in general, youth budgets are determined by the proportion of youth in a congregation, not the size of the church. And youth, on average, make up only 10 percent of a congregation.

Secondly, don't fall into the trap of thinking that your group is in competition with other churches. Instead, ask yourself how you're doing within *your own church*. "Why

First, He gives you the vision, then He gives you the PRO-vision.

don't I even have all of the kids that are in *my* church?" This is a good question for us all to ask.

When answering this question, first figure out what it's going to take to capture the hearts and attention of the kids in your church. But don't stop there. Begin to dream of all the other kids that God has called you to reach in your town. That's what building a dream is all about. Ask the Lord who He wants you to reach and how best to reach them. Remember that if you are only reaching the kids whose parents go to your church, you're not gaining any ground.

Once we have the dream, how, then, do we grow this thing? Philippians 4:19 says, "My God will meet all your needs according to his glorious riches in Christ Jesus." If you get God's vision, isn't it in His best interest to supply the needs for His dream? Do you think He is going to tease us and *not* give us His provision? Of course not!

DEVELOP A BUDGET FOR THE DREAM

Open your Bibles and turn with me to Luke 16. This parable of the shrewd manager is one of Jesus' most difficult parables. I have a real love/hate relationship with this passage. I love it because Jesus said it, but I hate it because the punch line in verse eight stings:

> *"The master commended the dishonest manager because he had acted shrewdly. For the people of this world are more shrewd in dealing with their own kind than are the people of the light."*
>
> —Luke 16:8

The master commended his steward not because he was dishonest, but because he was shrewd. This indicts most Christians. People of the world who make meaningless widgets are smarter with their money than the people in the kingdom of God. People who make toothpaste and soap put together better budgets than many ministries—and budgeting is about being shrewd. Sure, deciding sermon topics and the theme for this year is very important. But at some point we have to take the dream and reduce it down to how much it will cost. That's the work of a budget. There are two parts of a budget:

- *Operational costs* – These are ongoing costs that you want to keep as low as you can.
- *Capital costs* – These are one-time costs, like building a youth room or purchasing a sound system.

Do you think that having a large budget is something to brag about? It isn't. I believe in the "biggest bang for the buck"—the greatest number of souls for the fewest dollars. Your goal is to keep the operations and ongoing costs as low as possible. If, for example, you want a youth center, you must factor in how much it will cost each month—lights, bills, and rent. Lots of outreach attempts like this end up closing because no one thought about the monthly costs. Will businesses rally to support it? Will your pastor? A budget will help you project monthly costs.

In the midst of doing your budget let me encourage you to classify items as Needs versus Wants. Sometimes the things you think you *"need* to have" are really only a preference. They would be cool, but they're not necessary. Careful evaluation of ministry items in terms of need will help you stretch your budget dollar.

Go to the CD-ROM file titled "Funding Your Plan." Start planning your budget by filling out the first two pages.

Once you've figured out your one-time and ongoing needs, track your budget very closely—did you come in behind or ahead of budget? We do this at Teen Mania. I know this seems obvious, but many times people only think about ministry and not how to measure whether they stayed within budget. The crunch comes when the pastor comes in and says you're over budget, and you can't do it any-more. We must be more shrewd than most "people of the light."

I am a simple guy, but when my wife and I started Teen Mania over 20 years ago, we had a big dream. We didn't have any money, so we did what every ministry does: we wrote a letter to every person we knew—120 people. Every day we ran to the mailbox, just knowing that God would fill it with cash. But nobody sent anything!

We were reduced to living off the offerings of teenagers at the churches we'd visit (and there weren't many teenagers). We lived on a couple of hundred dollars a month. We stayed in people's homes and spent as little as we possibly could so we could buy some paper to print more letters and brochures. But even as we lived by faith, we were shrewd. We didn't rack up more expenses than we had money coming in.

The church cannot operate on the principle, "Oh, Lord, we will be able to keep the doors open as long as you send a generous donor this month." You won't hear Motorola or Proctor and Gamble say, "We hope people will buy this product and if they don't, we'll have to lay people off." They don't want to go out of business, so they plan ahead. They watch the economy. Sometimes they take financial risks, but only after they've researched them thoroughly. They are shrewd when the economy goes down and consider the long-term health of their organization. We must think the same way in our ministries.

Every budget needs to track the money coming in and the money going out. You know where the money will go *out*—that's your dream. You also need to figure out where the money will come *in*.

THE FOUR SOURCES OF MONEY

Teenagers. Some of you may think teenagers don't have money. Yet, the average teen spends $50 per week. Teens worldwide spend $100 billion per year.[1] They have money. Some earn it; some get it from their parents. But where do they spend it?

We put our money wherever we think it has value, so a ministry has to prove that it's worth a teenager's money. Otherwise, why would a teen want to give up his daily pizza, her designer jeans, or his movie tickets? Most teenagers have not been taught to give. You've all seen adults curl in the fetal position around their wallets when the senior pastor takes an offering. That attitude does not teach teenagers to give. When a mom hands her children a quarter or dollar to put in the collection plate, they don't learn giving; they are just transporting someone else's money!

We have to teach teens to be givers while they're young. The way you shape your kids now will have lifelong results. Teaching teens to be generous won't happen with one sermon; it is a continual education. Each week you

We put our money wherever we think it has value, so a ministry has to prove that it's worth a teenager's money.

It's no longer merely "throwing money in a bucket;" it's being part of a vision.

should take an offering and teach them a little bit about giving. Talk about Scripture verses that link generosity with God's blessing. Tell them of times God has blessed you when you have given for a big need. As Youth Specialists, we must raise up a generation of generous people.

Your dream must be clear to your teens. People are motivated to give when they see where their money is going. If you say, "We're going to build this youth center, and then we want to grow to 200 kids," they'll be excited to be a part of something. Think about the football coach who tells his team they're going to win the championship. They'll have to work hard, run until they drop, and practice six nights a week, and *they do it!* Every time you take an offering, give the vision. You've changed the value of your ministry in their eyes. Now they have to decide between spending money on pizza or changing their generation. It's no longer merely "throwing money in a bucket;" it's being part of a vision.

What can you tell them they'll receive in return? God will bless them. They'll get a sense of godly pride. They'll be excited to give money to Jesus to reach their generation.

Some of you might think I'm way too optimistic about teenagers' generosity. Yet, I can tell you story after story of youth pastors who have trained their group to give. For example, Scott Gurule's youth group (I'll be talking more about Scott and his group throughout the chapter) had 40 people when he started to teach them to give. In less than three years, the group grew to 400 people and the kids themselves gave the money; they didn't rely on fundraisers.

There are two ways you can raise money with your kids—doing fundraisers or teaching them to give. If they give, God will bless them, and they'll have more to give. They get better jobs and promotions. Mom and Dad bless them. The kids in Scott's youth group gave $55,000 their second year. They built a totally cool youth room. They couldn't wait to bring their friends to it, because it was *theirs*. They had ownership because they learned to give.

Teenagers are your first source of funds. Don't overlook them.

Parents. I really encourage you to have an ongoing relationship with the teens' parents—meet with them once a month, twice a month, whatever. Get them together, not just to take an offering, but to help them understand where you're going and what the dream is. Talk to them about the hot issues teens are dealing with. Talk to them about what you're preaching on for the next month or two. Give them your sermon notes in advance. (Wouldn't that be amazing if you actually prepared that far in advance?) "I just wanted you all to know what I'll be talking about, so when the kids come home, you can ask them about these things." A partnership with your kids' parents benefits everybody.

If you can have an upfront discussion with the parents about why you care for their kids and what you're going to do for them, it will knock them to the floor. Parents will appreciate being included, and they'll respect your plans.

Lay everything out for them. "Here is our vision—we want to have a youth room and double in size . . . You and your children stand to benefit the most from this ministry. Now, I know you already tithe to the church. But if you'd like to be a part of this vision and help not only your kids, but also the kids in this community, would you consider giving a one-time gift—or even an ongoing offering—in addition to what you're already giving? It's important, because the new vision and direction for this group will help your family directly."

I know youth pastors who have been very successful in generating offerings through the parents by making parents realize that youth ministry is not a Christian babysitting service. For this you must carry yourself like an adult, and not an overgrown teenager. If they think you're a goofy guy, they won't believe in your vision or fund it. They might throw a couple bucks at you, but you don't need a couple bucks. You've got a massive dream. You need some people to sell their boat, cash in some IRAs, or something big.

Do some comparison spending for them. Talk about the parents whose kid was having troubles, so they sent him to a psychologist for three years. That costs a ton of money, since insurance doesn't always cover psychiatric help. You're cheaper than a psychologist, and you're great preventive medicine!

So far, you've seen how you can get revenue from teens, from parents, and now (trust me; you're going to love me for this one) from outside sources.

Sources outside the church. We've been dream building, planning, and brainstorming. What kind of outside help does it take to accomplish your dream? Write down all the things you need and attach a price tag to them.

Now here's how you go about getting that price tag covered. On nice stationery write a little bit about your dream, all the things you need, and how much it's going to cost. Print copies of it and make sure they look good. Then carry that paper around with you EVERYWHERE you go. Day or night, don't leave home without it.

Then, when you get in conversations with people, and they ask you what you do, say, "Oh, I'm glad you asked. God's given me a heart for the young people of our region, and He's going to reach this generation. There are kids that are hurting and broken, and we're going to bus them off the streets." Whatever your vision is, don't be afraid to share it. "We're going to have vans and multi-media, and we'll pray for hurting kids and encourage them through our service."

You'll have to tailor your pitch depending on the person you're talking to. If he's not a Christian, you can still tell him the heart of what you're doing. Just don't use phrases like: "And the power of God . . ."! You don't have to express it like that. Simply say, "We're going to help a lot of hurting kids." Then share some stories or stats.

If you do this, you'll shock people into forwarding your dream. If you're walking around with a dream, you're weird. Most people don't have a dream and a vision of really doing something with their lives and helping a lot of other people. When they see you exuding this vision, they will be so enamored by what you're doing that they'll say, "Wow, that's awesome. Is there anything I can do to help?"

Trust me. People want to follow someone who's dedicated to a dream. People talk about leaders who have "charisma." They think it's something you're born with. But charisma is just a fancy word for someone who's "sold out for a dream." When people hear your well-thought-out and consuming dream, they'll want to help.

Help—a very interesting concept. People really care about kids; they just don't know what to *do*. When they find someone who knows what to do, they'll ask what they can do. You could say, "Well, just pray for us, brother." But is that all? Yes, you need prayer; you also need money. Instead say, "I'm glad you asked. As a matter of fact, I just happen to have a sheet right here that describes some things you could do to help. A bus, a van, a video projector, a PA system . . . would help. Lots of things would help because we care about these kids."

You're going to be talking to businesspeople. These people are mature and know how to run finances. They're impressed when they see someone who says more than, "I wanna reach kids." Anyone can say that. Instead, you say, "I want to reach kids, and I *know* how to reach them. I have a plan to do it. If I can just get these specific resources, then we can do *these* great things to help them." When business-people see your vision and plan, they'll be impressed with your ministry—and they will write you checks!

Here is a personal testimony. Once, I was meeting with the president of a corporation. I had heard that his compa-ny tithed and gave money to good causes and was hoping that subject would come up. If it didn't, maybe I could help it come up. So I asked him a bunch of questions, and at some point I said, "I heard your company tithes."

He said, "Well, as a matter of fact we do. We look for different needs and this and that . . . is there something going on?"

"Yeah, we're building dorms on our campus and reaching these kids." I went on describing my vision.

He said, "Well, maybe you could put something together and send it to me."

I instantly replied, "As a matter of fact . . ." and I pulled out the packet for him. He opened it and read all the charts and looked at the projections of how many kids we could reach. Then he turned it over and saw the exact needs we had—something like $700,000 to build a dormitory. He examined it all.

Finally he said, "Well, I can't commit to you now; I need to talk to the board of directors, but I'll tell you that we will do something." I was content; after all, something is bet-ter than nothing. About a month later he called me up and said he'd met with the board. "Remember your presenta-tion?" he asked. "We're sending you a check for $300,000."

Thank the Lord I just happened to have a packet to give to him that day. I'm telling you that it works when you get your vision together and make a nice-looking presentation.

So how do you meet these people? You knock on doors, or you go door-to-door to local businesses. Sometimes it just comes up with people you meet. Don't limit yourself to Christians. Even secular people want to help their community.

Sources within the church. This is usually the only place that pastors look for funds, yet this should really only be bonus money.

Let me tell you a little more about Scott Gurule, the youth pastor who taught his kids to give. He drew a line in the sand with his pastor. The church was giving him a budget of $500 a month. It was a church of about 2,000 people. He said, "We're never going to reach this whole community on $500 a month." (I know some of you are thinking you'd be very happy with $500 a month.) So he went to the pastor and said, "Thank you for your kindness, but why don't you give it to a missionary somewhere or some other charity. We're going to teach these kids how to give. They're going to reach their own generation."

He taught his youth to give, they gave, and their group grew tenfold. So, if you get money from inside the church, terrific. That can be bonus money; but don't think that your whole destiny depends on whether the church is generous or the pastor decides to put youth ministry in the budget. God will fund His own dream.

On page three of the CD-ROM file "Funding," dream about how you are going to begin pulling in and tracking the revenue you need.

Regardless of where you find your funding—from one

of these sources, or a combination of them all—there is one overriding thing you must do.

SUBMIT YOUR BUDGET TO YOUR PASTOR

Submit everything to your pastor—your dream, your vision, your goals, and even your budget plans. Don't go to anyone to ask for donations until your pastor is onboard and behind your ministry. Tell him your dream and vision and make sure they are in harmony with the church's vision. If they aren't, then you need to rethink them and make sure there is full agreement.

You need to get your pastor and the people in your church excited about reaching kids. "How can I help them catch the vision?" you ask. Understand this: people care about young people; they just don't know how to help. People who aren't even saved care about young people. I have seen grown men cry and say they want to help young people, but they just don't know what to do. You need to show them *how* you plan to do it.

First, you tell them stories of real-life broken kids who are hurting. Don't just go in and say, "Pastor, we want to do this huge thing that's never been done before. What do you think?" Be wise.

Instead say, "Pastor, I've really been thinking about the young people in our community. You know Josh Taylor, the young man who is dealing with . . . ? My heart really goes out to him. And I just found out this week that a dozen girls in the local school are pregnant. My heart would like to do something to help them too. What do you think, Pastor?" Help him see the lives that are really hurting. "Did you know about the kid who tried to commit suicide? Maybe there's something we could do . . . "

Stories open people's hearts to help. Once your pastor asks what he can do, then you can share the vision of opening a youth center or a place where kids could come each

Wednesday that they wouldn't be ashamed of. Don't present it as a big thing that *you* want to do, but as your understanding of God's heart for these kids. Don't expect it to happen all at once. Share a couple of ideas at a time. Allow your pastor to grow with the plan. Make sure he is in agreement before you go and get your money.

One last thing: I encourage you *not* to ignore this stuff about budgeting. I know a lot of youth pastors hate talking about money. "Wouldn't it be great if we could just have the dream, and someone else gave us the money?" No, this is the wrong attitude.

Budgeting is the leader's job. You have to have the dream *and* find the resources. It's not an added burden for youth ministry; it's one of the many parts of youth ministry. If we care about kids, we must find a way to reach them. Part of that way is finding the resources. When a person wants to start a business, she doesn't say, "If only I had the money." No, she puts together a plan and finds a way to finance her business—she borrows from Uncle Ted, or goes to a venture capitalist.

Now is the time to start budgeting. Use page four of the CD-ROM file "Funding" to help you get started.

Our business is touching lives, and we must find resources as well. Our commitment means we will find the resources

Submit everything to your pastor—your dream, your vision, your goals, and even your budget plans.

Budgeting is the leader's job. You have to have the dream and find the resources.

to finance the dream. Without the resources, the dream will never become reality. Lives will never be saved or changed.

I know a youth ministry in which the youth pastor started with 26 kids, and a year later he had 260 kids. He created a center right on the church grounds without receiving one cent from the church. They raised all $66,000 by doing the very things that we've talked about here. It was an incredibly cool place complete with video games and a café. You too can accomplish dreams this big.

We'll close this chapter on *Funding Your Plan* by looking again at the example of Scott Gurule, the youth pastor in Tucson, Arizona.

> *Scott Gurule taught his youth group to give. And give they did. As they became generous and gave, God began to bless them. They grew in numbers from 40 to 400 in just three years, and raised $120,000 in about a year without selling candy bars or washing cars. They built their own youth room and bought sound and lights, which in turn helped to facilitate their vision to reach more teens.*

Let's look at some of the key things Scott taught his group that convinced them to be generous. You will discover exactly what he did to mobilize them, and you can implement these same principles in your youth ministry. Watch God do incredible things through your young people as they learn how to be givers.

When Scott started as a youth pastor in Tucson, the

church gave him a budget of $500 a month to run a youth group. But God had given Scott a vision for a youth *ministry*, and he knew there was no way he could build the thriving youth ministry he had in his heart on that amount.

Youth *ministries* (some call them youth churches) are self-supported (youth *groups* are supported). You have to sow before you grow, go, or glow. Think about it. Teens spend over three billion dollars a year to buy balls for sports. Girls spend over seven billion dollars a year on make-up and clothing. They *have* money to spend.

So Scott began to build the values of giving and generosity into his group. He talked about all the different offerings in Scripture. He showed them what God had to say about the practices and attitudes of giving offerings in the Old and New Testament. When he taught the young people how to sacrifice, and the difference between a tithe and a sacrificial offering, they went nuts.

God is looking for a generation of givers! We have to change the way things are done. People may have different thoughts on how tithing should work, but we cannot escape the fact that we are called to tithe of our firstfruits.

These are some of the things Scott instilled into his students:

- *No loud offerings* – We shouldn't tip God like He's a cosmic bellboy. Don't throw in quarters unless that really is the best you can give. Scott refused to do car washes or candy sales to raise money. Those are paltry things. God has put wealth in this generation, and the shrewd manager will use the wealth. Some of the youth who didn't have any money put their drugs in the plate, because that was all they had. God won't release what is in His hand until you release what is in yours. Scott's adult leaders were required to be givers to set an example. Tithing and sacrificial offering became the name of the game. The youth ministry last year gave $58,900 with 400 kids.

- *Give up something* – Teach young people to fast. He asked them to give up their snack food to fast and pray. This gave them the money to tithe into the youth ministry. These kids have money and his youth budget was proof of it. He said, "Next year we're going to have a youth conference, and it will be free because you all will finance it." They got behind it and they did.

As a Youth Specialist, you have to be prepared to change your kids' and your church's attitudes. Demand more of them, and they will step up to the challenge. Don't be wishy-washy about money just because "youth guys" hate to talk about money. You are a Youth Specialist, and you will do whatever it takes to achieve God's dream.

1. Zollo, Peter, "The Cosmetics Category: Talking to Teens," American Demographics, November 1995, http://www.ecrmepps.com/Expose/V3_3/V3_3_A8.asp (accessed October 25, 2005).

CHAPTER SIX

Building Your Dream Team

Why do you need people to assist you in the vision? Some of you already know why: *"Because I'm gonna die if I don't get help!"* One of the main reasons youth pastors wear themselves out is that once they get their vision, they try to do it all themselves. We all know the old saying, "If you want something done right, you've got to do it yourself," and that's what too many of us try to do. The truth is, we can only do it by ourselves for a little while before we're delirious and our family falls apart. I believe we can have a healthy family and a great ministry at the same time, but the key to having both is to surround ourselves with a team who will buy into the vision and

If you think you can accomplish the vision by yourself, then your vision is not big enough.

pour their guts out to bring it to fruition. A *dream team* of adult volunteers and teenagers around us will help us accomplish the vision.

I can hear you object: "It probably is better to work with a team, but it's so hard to feel like you're always begging people for help." Let me assure you, it's infinitely harder to achieve God's dream by yourself. Let's look at this issue a little closer.

WHY DO I NEED A TEAM?

Because this vision is bigger than you are. If you think you can accomplish the vision by yourself, then your vision is not big enough. I talk a lot about vision and building ministry because I believe that *Jesus didn't die for 10 quality people, He died for the world.* It doesn't matter how big your church is, or how big your town is—*your ministry can and must grow.* Why do we need workers? Our vision demands it. It will take a lot of work to reach this generation, and we need help.

Because your group will grow. This is a good thing. You want your group to get to the point where you *can't* handle them all. Your ministry will generate a variety of roles for adult volunteers to assume. You've got to raise up a group of people willing to help administrate different parts of the vision. It's not just about you and a group anymore. Once this thing starts growing, you have to have people who are willing to roll up their sleeves and get in the trenches. The good news is that when people see a vision in progress, they're eager to help. And you'll need every one of them.

Because the vision harnesses people's energy. As we mentioned earlier, Proverbs 29:18 tells us that God's people need a vision to harness their energy. Without vision, people cast off restraint. You know this is true. You've seen what happens when kids have no vision from God to bridle their energy—they get into sports, drama, choir, drugs, or gangs . . . with a passion! Adults aren't much different; they just do other things with their energy—take a second job or work hours of overtime to buy a bigger house or bigger car or bigger something else. We have a ton of believers sitting in church with no vision from God to harness their energy; instead they let the world harness their energy. If they are going to use their energy somewhere, it should be used for the kingdom of God. So in a very real way, though they don't even know it, they have a need. *They need to have their energy harnessed.*

I want to show you how to build your dream team. What kind of people do you want to choose? What kind of people don't you want to choose? Let's break it down.

WHO SHOULDN'T YOU CHOOSE FOR THE TEAM?

Somebody is better than nobody, right? Wrong. You don't want to get just anybody who will say yes. You want

When people see a vision in progress, they're eager to help. And you'll need every one of them.

handpicked people. A bad volunteer can bring poison to your group that will hurt your ministry, not help it.

You may already have inherited bad volunteers because they were already in place when you got there. Now you're stuck with them. Here's what you don't want in a team member:

Adults who always compare you to the last youth group leader. Can you imagine if everybody had kept complaining to Joshua, "Moses always used to do it *this* way"? You do not need people like that. You might justify their involvement because they've volunteered in youth ministry for 10 or 20 years. But if they're stuck in how it's always been done, they'll never hear your vision for how it *could* be done.

You might think, "At least they're helping," but are they really? It only takes one person pulling in the other direction to ruin all your momentum. You will try to get people fired up, but they will be sucked back down with "how it used to be."

People who are disloyal. People who are disloyal agree with everything to your face, but then you hear that they are saying other things behind your back. You simply cannot operate with that. It's unacceptable under any circumstances.

Adults who have their own dreams for youth ministry. As you look for a team to assist you with your vision, you will sometimes find people with a vision of their own. They'll say, "I always thought that we should do this or that." They'll have their own ideas of what the youth ministry *ought* to do and what direction it should take. *There is room for only one vision at a time.*

Some might think it's arrogant for a youth pastor to

say, "We only need to have *this* vision." No, it's not arrogant; this is how God does things throughout the Bible. He chooses one person, a man or a woman, gives him or her a dream, then gathers people around that leader to support the dream and vision. The leader doesn't call a committee, and he doesn't vote on things. These are godly principles.

People might bring baggage from a previous youth group: "We always voted on things like this, and I think we should go in that direction." You should respond with, "That's fine, God bless you; go start a ministry and do that. I don't want to stifle you at all. In fact I want you to be free to do those things." You don't have to fire anybody, just set them free. "But he's a deacon," you say. Oh, well, that's a different story. Now, obviously, you'll need to get your pastor's support to set him free. The point is that you can't have a bunch of nay-sayers pulling you back.

Yes, you need a team to volunteer and support you but you need them to support *you*—not their own agendas. Their role will be to help you brainstorm how to make the dream that God has given you into a reality.

Remember, for whatever reason, the adult with a dream of her own is not the leader of the youth ministry; God chose you. Before you came, the pastor could have chosen her, but he didn't. For whatever reason, God didn't think she was ready yet. If He had, she would have had the opportunity to implement her own vision.

If you find people like this, and they are not able to support your vision with word and deed, you will have to let them go. If you don't, they'll try to run your whole ministry. For whatever reason, these adults are not leaders of their own youth ministries; God chose you.

Remember the example of Absalom, in 2 Samuel 15:2. While his father, David, was king, Absalom sat outside the gate and said: "You know, if I were king, I'd do things differently," and, "If I were king, I'd fix this or that."

Eventually it split the kingdom. If you have an Absalom in your group, it will prevent you from doing effective ministry. You don't want this. *"Someone" is not better than no one in this case.*

People with too much extra time on their hands. You might think this doesn't make sense. Don't people with extra time have more time for ministry? Here's the problem. There's usually a reason they have so much extra time. *Nobody else wants them either.*

The people who don't have any time, *they* are the people you want, because they are the people that *everybody else wants.* Everyone else wants them because they get the job done. They make things happen! Your job is to prove to them how your dream and your vision are more important than all the other things that they've been asked to commit to.

Because these are productive people, even if they give you only a little bit of time, it'll be more valuable than somebody who gives you a lot of time but doesn't have the right motivation. These individuals have to constantly be reminded, pumped up, and asked over and over again to do things. By the time you've told them 10 times how to do the job, you could have done it yourself.

"Why didn't anybody tell me this before?" you ask. "You've just described three people on my team! Now what do I do?" If I have been describing people in your group of adult helpers, then you may need to start thinking about how to release them from your ministry.

How to "set free" adults who don't help your ministry. I have never fired anybody, but I have had to set some people free. Always give people a chance to change problem behavior (and be thankful when they take it). Giving them that chance means you must be willing to confront them. Then, if they don't change, you have to confront them again and get even tougher. Few people enjoy confrontation. I don't like it. It's not natural for me to confront, but I recognize that confrontation is part of leadership, and, when people respond positively, it can be the catalyst for positive life-changes.

So give them the chance. Explain the vision. Explain how their behavior doesn't move it forward. Be as positive as you can, and then watch them. Some will make changes but I guarantee there will be others who won't respond. Oh sure, they'll say they will, but before long you'll see the issue crop up again, and at some point you'll have to direct them to express their energy and desire to minister in another way.

Let's be clear on this issue: this isn't being mean. You've given them the chance to respond, and it's godly for them to be loyal and learn submission. If they can't or won't, then you can't keep struggling with them forever. Love is more than mere kindness. Kindness tries not to hurt anybody's feelings, regardless of truth. Love demands honesty, spoken as gently as possible. Your goal is to move toward your dream, and to speak the truth in love as you release these people from a dead-end situation.

WHO SHOULD YOU CHOOSE FOR THE TEAM?

Now, let's look for the *right* qualities in leaders. Paul reminds Timothy of these very traits when he says, "And the things you have heard me say in the presence of many witnesses entrust to reliable men who will also be qualified to teach others" (2 Tim. 2:2). What is the first characteristic Paul finds so important in men who are going to teach others?

Qualified. First, they need to be qualified. They need to have an ability—a talent—for something. This means you must be discriminating about the people you

Your goal is to move toward your dream, and to speak the truth in love.

pick for different parts of your ministry. Just because someone wants to help, doesn't mean they should. Too often we enlist people who don't have any talent and let them lead worship anyway. Then we wonder why we have bad worship!

I remember when I was first saved in high school. I was learning to play the guitar and was always begging to lead a song during worship. I was terrible, my voice was rotten, and so they never let me.

I'm so glad they kept saying no. It forced me to practice more, which was a good thing. But it also helped me realize that music wasn't my calling. We're not all good at everything. I'm not saying that your helpers need to be perfect at the things you're looking for. You can train them and they can improve, but they need at least some aptitude before you throw them into a position outside their skill sets.

Consider making some kind of application form that includes an inventory of skills and abilities, so you can assess a person's experience. If, for example, a woman writes for her company newsletter, she may be a good writer for fliers and brochures. Find out each person's experience, and match his or her skills to the roles you need.

Faithful. You've got to find somebody who's a faithful Christian. You want someone of proven Christian character. You don't want somebody who just started coming to church. 1 Timothy 3 tells us that a leader "must not be a recent convert" and "must first be tested." You need to know that they've been faithful in their walk with God and are deep in the Lord. It scares me sometimes that churches don't do enough of a background check on people. It's wonderful that they're really excited about God, but if they've only been saved a couple of months, what happens if they fall away? Do you realize what that could do to your kids? Everything you've been working for could be blown away.

I see this problem in Christian music. A talented band signs with a label, but they don't have a proven track record of faithfulness. Then, when they become famous, their character falls short; they blow it, fall away, and their fans are disillusioned with the faith. We need to look for people who are faithful and strong.

We need to be careful not to cheapen what faithfulness means. Faithfulness is more than perfect church attendance every week. It is pursuing God, reading the Word, living true to God's promises and convictions, and growing in faith.

Besides their faithfulness to the Lord, will your leaders faithfully represent *you*? When an artist paints a portrait, the best compliment you can give him is that it's a *faithful representation*. When you talk about leaders—your dream team—they need to faithfully represent you, your heart for kids, and your heart for God. Whether it's on a Wednesday night, or all of the rest of the week, if they're part of your team, they have to represent you well.

Equally yoked. Your Dream Team should be "equally yoked." My interpretation of "equally yoked" means we are on the same wavelength.

If, for example, you cast the vision to your leaders, "I want 100 kids in this group this year, 200 next year, 400 the year after, and we want to save a generation!"—your leaders should be on the same page as you are. But if your leaders say, "As long as we have 10 on-fire kids, we're

Faithfulness is more than perfect church attendance every week. It is pursuing God, reading the Word, living true to God's promises and convictions, and growing in faith.

pretty good with that," you're definitely still family in Christ, but you are *not equally yoked.*

Or, let's say you are passionate about breathing life into young people so that they can save their own generation, but your team thinks the best you can hope for is that they don't have sex or do drugs. You are *not equally yoked.*

What we're talking about here is philosophy of ministry, what you're passionate about. You will not always readily find people who are equally yoked, and at times you may have to breathe some of that into them. That's okay. They'll change. Ultimately, though, you've got to be equally yoked with your dream team.

Good character. You can see in 1 Timothy 3 that God wants leaders to have character. In fact, He is more serious about that than we are. When you're a leader you can help a lot of people, but you can also hurt a lot of people. The more opportunity you have to help, the more opportunity you have to hurt. Look at the example of Moses.

Remember, he was leading the children of Israel, a group of about three million. Some youth group, huh? The group was thirsty, so God said, "*Speak* to the rock." And what did Moses do? He *struck* it in his anger, and as a result, God wouldn't let him go into the promised land. There's a huge principle behind this thing. God expected Moses to behave better than that. If Moses was going to be in charge of the group, he needed to be a trustworthy leader—not one who was ruled by his attitudes and impulses.

The same principle holds true for leaders in youth ministry. God is looking for people with character and self-control. He demands a high level of character and holiness in the small things and big things in their lives.

Take some time now to think about the names of some people you might want on your leadership team. Go to your computer and open the CD-ROM file titled "Dream Team," and begin to list those names as you prayerfully consider each one.

HOW TO RECRUIT THEM

Now that you've spotted the kind of people you want, with the qualifications you need, how do you get them to sign up?

Pray. But pray discerningly. Write out the job description and then ask God, "Who would be the best person for *this* role?" Even if they don't know you're praying about them—even if they don't know you want them—write their names on your flow chart. "I want this person for this, and this person for this." Pray, "God, give me the opportunity to talk to them, because I know that they've done these kinds

God is looking for people with character and self-control.

of things in the past and they'd probably be good at this."
Then pray for Him to open their hearts to helping you. Once
you've done this, you can approach them.

Do not just ask them if they will help you with the
youth group. As we've talked about before, these people are
busy; they need to see a reason to spend their precious time
on your ministry.

Don't forget you're looking to build a "dream team,"
not just an hour-a-week babysitting service. You need to get
to know these people yourself before you recruit them. For
both of these reasons, your next step is . . .

Get to know them. Maybe you don't know them that
well. This is okay. You don't always want to ask your clos-
est friends to help with everything. You need to get other
people involved in your ministry for it to grow. So take
them out to lunch, interact in a social setting, etc. Start with
small talk, but be ready to move on to your purpose.

Share your vision. After you've gotten to know them,
say something like, "I've got some things on my heart I'd
like to share with you and see what you think." Don't be
afraid to get passionate. This is like fundraising. Just as people will contribute money to someone with a huge dream,
these people will be more likely to volunteer if you are excited about what you're doing.

Explain why they're important. Once you've shared
your dream with them, get specific about how you see their
role. Tell them the strengths you see, and why you think
they would be vital to the vision.

You don't even need to ask them to commit to "until
death do us part." Just ask for a short-term commitment. "If
you could help me for three weeks in this area," or "just two
months over here." Hopefully they'll say, "Sure!" Then once
they are done with the three weeks or two months, you can

get together again and say, "Well, you've done a great job, you've really become part of the team. Do you feel the Lord's calling you to keep going?" Either God will touch their hearts for young people, or they'll have learned that youth ministry isn't where they're called to be. Either way, it's a win-win situation.

Ask them to help the teens, not to help you! It's hard to ask people, "Will you help me out?" But if you're talking about the kids, and the vision of reaching more of them, that's a lot easier, isn't it? This isn't about you. Point the focus away from you and more toward the vision. Your goal for these leaders is first, for them to get a heart for the kids, and second, for them to embrace your vision. After a trial period, they should be incredibly excited about what you're doing.

Don't feel like you have to settle for just anyone who will show up. You will find a whole army of people with a heart for the kids and a willingness to embrace your vision. So keep praying for God to raise up the leaders that you'll need for your dream and your vision.

TURNING THEM INTO A TEAM

Just because you've gotten your leaders to show up doesn't make them useful. It's what you *do* with them once you have them that will make them useful. Compare it to a sports team. The 2004 U.S. Men's Olympic Basketball Team had a lot of star players on it, but there was no teamwork. So they lost. They lost to a bunch of teams with mediocre players and great teamwork. Where does teamwork come from? The coach. In this case, you. Once you've assembled your team, don't worry about how impressive they may or may not seem from the get-go. You are going to pull them together into something fantastic. What does it take for a team to become a dream team?

You will find a whole army of people with a heart for the kids and a willingness to embrace your vision.

A vision for themselves as a group. You've already given your team a glimpse of your vision for youth ministry. You've answered their questions: How big will it be? What's the nature of our youth ministry? What has God put on our heart?

Now you have to share your vision for the team. *What is this team about?* Just like a coach, you have to create the atmosphere in which this team will work. Here are some good examples of what any ministry team should be about.

We'll have fun together. It's not going to be all work. Ministry needs to be enjoyable. This doesn't just mean, "Okay, let's all play a game." But your focus must be more than, "Did you do this job? Did you do this job?" Ministry is about more than just getting the job done; it's about having fun while you're doing the job. The relationships you build are part of the vision. "You know what, this is the kind of team we're going to be: the kind that has fun together." When a team has fun together, it creates energy. We'll talk about that more a little later.

We'll be competent. One person is good at one thing, and another is good at something else. We'll all do our jobs well, and together we'll make this a great team. That includes pulling together toward the same vision. As a leader, you don't need to stress that they be loyal to *you*, but that they be loyal to God's vision for the group, as revealed to you because the end of that vision is people; it's lives.

You're asking them to get sold out for the vision and pursue it with excellence.

We'll be a community of trust. The meaning of trust here is two-fold. First, there is the sense of sharing the same basic values of honesty and integrity—which we can almost take for granted. But trust also deals with having confidence in each other to fulfill different roles. It's not about who gets a certain position. We are different members of the body of Christ, and each of us will serve in different ways. We don't ask, "How come he's in front more than I am? How come they get to do *that* ministry?" It will take some problem solving. The team has to work together to figure out how to get something done and maximize everybody's gifts.

I would definitely recommend that you and your team go do team-building events together—high ropes, obstacle courses, etc. These events help your team to bond and build trust and learn how to operate as a team. You can look in the phone book or call some different camps.

We'll challenge each other. This is an environment of stretching each other without threatening each other. Ideas will come from different people. An idea can be discussed, modified, or ultimately rejected. People need to be affirmed, and never rejected. This means that people can't afford to identify themselves with their ideas. You'll be doing lots of brainstorming with your team, and lots of things will be thrown out there. We want to challenge the way we think, not who we are. We're just trying to refine our ideas and make each other better. Amen?

We'll personally care about each other. We will get the job done, but not at the expense of each other. We don't just care about the vision; we care about each other as we walk toward the vision. We care about each other's personal growth. Are we really growing in the Lord, or are we

When a team has fun together, it creates energy.

just kind of strung out and barely having quiet times ourselves? People need to commit to each other enough to look each other in the eye and say, "Hey, what's really going on? How's your family doing? How's your walk with God going?"

As the leader, it's your job to cultivate this atmosphere. Start the process by spending a little one-on-one time with them. It's so easy for them to feel that all you want out of them is their hard work and time. You need to go the extra mile to show that you care about them. Maybe you don't know someone that well; maybe you inherited her from the last youth pastor; maybe he was forced on you. Doesn't matter. Be prepared to invest yourself in their lives.

IDENTIFY THE PURPOSE OF THE TEAM

Vision and purpose are two different things. The vision means what kind of team you're going to be—your "atmosphere." Purpose means, "Why are we here? What will we accomplish?" You must define purpose. Well, the purpose is to accomplish the vision. How do you do that? You have to work.

But work on what? The purpose of your team, essentially, is to figure out how to accomplish the vision, and then do it. Each person you invite onto the team needs to be able to see where he or she fits into the vision. For example, is she on the drama team or does she lead praise and worship? If you achieve your dream, it will be because your leaders did the work behind it.

Take the next few minutes to define your team's purpose. Use page two of the CD-ROM file "Dream Team" to guide you.

Some leaders are not very secure and want to get all the credit. A confident, well-balanced leader doesn't care who gets the glory. It's not about you. It's not about your individual leaders. It's about God and His dream.

It's such an empty feeling to have a victory all by yourself. An Olympic runner who had won several gold medals was asked, "Of all the gold medals that you've won, which one was the sweetest?" She said that it was the one relay for which she won a gold medal. "But why?" She answered, "Because I got to share the victory with three others."

Ministry isn't about glory. It's about creating a team with whom you can share the victory. It's "we," not "me." They're there to assist, advise, and labor with you.

This is the purpose of your team—figuring out the "how" of the vision.

DEFINE CLEAR EXPECTATIONS

Laying out the expectations helps to define the relationships of each team member. You need to be clear about the expectations you have of them. They need to be clear of the expectations they can have from you. If you don't clarify expectations, your team will always let you down, because they didn't even know what you were expecting of them. Here are some possible expectations:

Count the cost before they join the team. They're not just coming to show up. "We're about building a vision, building a ministry, reaching a whole generation and I'm going to need your heart, I'm going to need your sweat, I'm

Ministry isn't about glory. It's about creating a team with whom you can share the victory.

going to need your time. I need you here. I'm expecting that when you committed, you counted the cost. And I will not keep begging you to do this." Before a recruit enlists in the army, he's a volunteer. After he enlists, he's committed. It needs to be the same in youth ministry. You can still show compassion and understanding, but raise the bar on expectations.

Have an active walk with God. Your team needs to have its quiet time and grow in the Lord. Members need to keep a strong walk with God. They need to be faithful. Yes, this means faithful attendance, but more than that, they need to faithfully represent you. There is another very realistic expectation: expecting your team to read and to grow in God.

Bring work to the table. People often think the only time they have to work is at the meeting. "I'm showing up, isn't that enough?" No. I need you to work in between meetings. Maybe it's research, maybe it's planning, maybe it's making phone calls about the projects that we're working on. Meetings should become times where you discuss the work that's already been done. You're not there to babysit them. "Did you do your work? Please come back!" You shouldn't have to call them a million times to make sure the work gets done.

Other expectations for meetings: be on time; bring your best; be ready to think; be bright and alert; contribute.

Communicate with you. You know there shouldn't be any logjams. If something's not going to work out, then your team needs to e-mail, call, or let you know as soon as possible. Most of us have a pager, cell phone, or answering machine. When you figure out communication within your own ministry, it will diffuse 90 percent of all the confusion.

WHAT SHOULD THEY EXPECT FROM YOU?

These are the things you should be able to tell your team:

I will be the leader. "I will take responsibility." "I will set the standard." "The buck stops with me." "I am the leader."

I'm going to keep my heart with God right. Tell them, "I'm not going to be two-faced with you; you're going to see the real me. I'm not going to pretend everything is great when I'm digging myself up from the bottom of the pit. I will be sincere with you." Some things that go unspoken shouldn't go unspoken. Tell them to hold you accountable. "You can ask me anytime, 'Are you growing in the Lord?' If I'm growing, I'll tell you; if I'm not, I'll thank you for getting me back on track."

I will help you. "You know, you may not get everything right. That's fine. If you mess something up, I will coach you through it. I'm going to help you get better and as a result you'll make more of an impact on lives." That's what it's about. Helping your leaders make an impact on lives. A lot of people feel insecure and don't think they can really help. Suddenly, when they're part of your team, they'll be able to do a lot of things. Why? Because you believe in them and help them grow.

When you have questions, you can expect to hear back from me. You're not just going to go into an endless spin. "What about this, what about this?" Expect to hear back from me. I will respond to your questions. When you have a cry for help, you don't know what to do, you have a question, you can expect me to respond. You'll hear back from me when you have a question.

I'm going to be an encouragement to you. "I'm going to inspire and encourage you." One of the great coaches said, "My job is to get guys to do what they hate doing, so they can become what they've always wanted to become." There will be times when your leaders are frustrated and discouraged. You will help them through those times. We all have to do that. We all have to do things that we don't like doing so much, because it helps us to do the things that we really love doing: seeing lives changed.

Make these things clear. These are your guidelines for your team and for yourself. With these principles of leadership and teamwork in place, you have the foundation for a healthy team.

CHAPTER SEVEN

Leading Your Dream Team

So, you have the group, you've given them the vision, the purpose, and you've clarified the expectations. What do you actually do when you meet? What can you do to make this team proficient? To make it a high performance dream team? Well, let me give you some detailed things to actually do.

BEFORE THE MEETINGS

You need to prepare. This is the biggest challenge for leaders: we have to prepare for meetings. We all know we need to prepare to preach, but how many times do we excuse ourselves from preparing for a meeting with our

Thinking like a leader is about more than just getting these people to do a job. It's about pouring into their lives.

team? "Oh, this is just a small group meeting," we say. Listen carefully. You probably need to prepare more for those meetings than for preaching, because the impact you have on your team in a meeting will have a greater impact than any of your sermons. You're shaping the team who's building the ministry.

What do I mean prepare? Ask, what do I need to bring to the table to make sure it's worth the team's time? I've told them to come to the meeting prepared. To honor their time, I also must be prepared.

Make a deposit. Don't ever meet without depositing value into your leaders. The temptation is to think logistics and nothing else: "We've got a retreat in a month. Who's driving the bus? Who's doing this or that?" If that's all you focus on, you'll drain them dry.

Thinking like a leader is about more than just getting these people to do a job. It's about pouring into their lives. The more you personally deposit into them, the more they'll love you, the more loyal they'll be, and the more they'll feel like a better person around you. Not only is this good for your leaders, it will bear great interest in a heart for ministry. What else can you do to prepare for the meeting?

Prepare for the work that needs to be done. Think about how you are going to run your meeting. You need an agenda or a format that is more than just, "Here's a pile of work, okay, let's attack!" You need to decide what are the priority issues to cover at this meeting. In what order should they be discussed? What are the decisions that need to be made? At our meetings, we try to think about one work item at a time, and think it through together with time for each person to bring ideas to the table. Then we take a break and tackle the next area.

As we've mentioned before, part of preparing for the meeting is making sure that everyone else brings their homework—research items that you've assigned them beforehand. You can schedule a meeting for every day of the week, but if people haven't done their homework and brought it to the table, then you won't have a productive meeting.

Make sure you have the authority to get the job done. If you're meeting about something specific, and you've spent a lot of time planning for it, you'll want to be sure that you've got the authority from your pastor to tell your team, "Go with it." If you don't, you'll end up wasting your time and a lot of other people's time.

Be strategic about who attends the meeting. Is everybody who's necessary to get the job done present at the meeting? Do you have some people attending who don't really need to be there? Make some phone calls, e-mail, and cover your bases so that the work doesn't get hung up because a key person is missing.

Where and when is the meeting scheduled? When you schedule a meeting, you want to bring forth the best from

The more you build as a team, the more proficient your team will be and the quicker you'll get to your vision.

your people. So if it's going to be a three-hour meeting, you don't want to cram everyone into the back of your VW. Find a place where you will have something to write on, and an environment that produces creativity. If you want high productivity, you'll also want to consider when you will schedule the meeting. Will some people need to leave early? What time will they be the most focused?

Go to your computer and open up again to the CD-ROM file titled "Dream Team." Use pages three and four to help you prepare before each dream team meeting.

DURING THE MEETING

Be psyched. My goal for every meeting that I lead is to have people walk in the door and say, "This is the best place in the world to be. I don't want to be a part of any other ministry. I love being here." Amen! They ought to be so hyped. Not because you said, "Isn't this a great place?" but because they see the vision and they know it's going to happen. "We're going to reach 50 kids next month, and then next year we're going to have 100, and it's going to grow." It's incredible for them to walk out feeling, "Man, I love this place; this place rocks."

It's not easy getting them to that place. They'll see the size of your big vision and think, "Man, this is hard." But anything that's worthwhile is hard, right? So you make it a fun place to be. You give them space to use their energy to change the world and change people's lives. You give them a reason to say, "I wouldn't want to be any other place in the world."

Sometimes getting to that place will be tied to the vision, but it will also be tied to the team. I love the people. We work hard and change lives. Your team will be productive when they begin to love the people they're doing ministry with as much as they love the vision. How does this happen?

Plan team-building time. Earlier, we mentioned the importance of fun, team-building time. Your job as a leader is not just building the ministry; it's about building relationships, too. Listen carefully. The more you build as a team, the more proficient your team will be and the quicker you'll get to your vision. Let me give you some examples on how this works.

You don't have to spend a lot of money to build a team. You can eat together or go out to play laser tag. Go dirt biking, camping, or ride horses. There are all kinds of low-cost relationship-building things you can do.

Let me tell you about one of the first times I did this. I was just starting to understand that we weren't supposed to just work, we also needed to have some fun and have relationships. So, I e-mailed my leadership team in the ministry and said, "Listen, there's a lot of construction down on the campus and we need to get out there with some of those construction workers and just relate to them. So, bring some

My goal for every meeting that I lead is to have people walk in the door and say, "This is the best place in the world to be."

There's something about the synergy that happens when you have fun together.

work clothes; we're going to get dirty together." I'm sure my team was thinking, "What is going on with Ron? He's lost it. We have to run a whole ministry and he wants us to . . . uh, okay, whatever."

So they brought their old clothes to the next all-day planning meeting that we do once a month. They didn't wear them; they just brought them. When everyone was there I said, "We'll just spend part of the day just getting out there and relating, so I have a project that I want us to work on. Follow me." They all followed me out of the conference room into a warehouse and opened the door. In the warehouse was a bunch of different dirt bikes and four-wheelers that I had rented. Their eyes opened wide, and I have never seen people leave to change their clothes so fast! Our property in Garden Valley has about 470 acres, and we went out and we rode those dirt bikes through the mud and dirt for hours. We tipped over, we went over jumps, we laughed, and we got disgustingly dirty. We had so much fun, and took a video and pictures of it all. About noon we were done, went and took showers, and had lunch together.

That afternoon we met and I'm telling you, we had a legendary meeting. We came up with some of the most creative, breakthrough ideas that we have ever had in the ministry. There's something about the synergy that happens when you have fun together. You're laughing, you're trusting, you're sending the signal, "I don't just care about you for the work that you bring to the table; I care about you as a person, and we're gonna be a team in this thing." It was a landmark day in all our minds.

Since then, we've done a lot of other team-building kinds of things. We've hunted together, gone to sports events together, and lots of things that are just kind of off the scale and strange. Recently, we went to the jungle in Ecuador together and visited some tribal people. Some of you may remember back in the 1950s, Jim Elliot and a few missionaries were martyred by the Auca Indians in Ecuador. We actually got to meet the Indians who killed them. It was an incredible experience that none of us will ever forget.

You don't have to leave the country to have legendary opportunities for team-building. You don't even have to leave your town. Do be intentional about finding things that build relationships. When you build that kind of trust and synergy into relationships, you'll get the kind of inspired planning meetings we've been talking about here. All it takes is one idea—one amazing, anointed idea—to break through a lot of the red tape, a lot of the reasons you didn't think you could get there. That's what your planning is about, right? How to get there.

Do whatever you have to do to cultivate an environment for your team that will generate those ideas. It will be worth any money that you spend on the trip, or that outing, or that dinner together, or whatever it is. It is a great investment. Team-building makes ministry a lot more fun, but it also helps you get to your vision quicker.

The power of "What if." As we talked about in earlier chapters, you need to rally your team around the vision and the planning to accomplish it. Don't be afraid to think big,

Team-building makes ministry a lot more fun, but it also helps you get to your vision quicker.

amazing goals, to think outside the box, to think, *"What if we . . . "* There's a lot of power in *what if* thinking. *"What if* this is what God is saying?"

This is exactly what I did when we first pondered going to the Silverdome: *"What if* we filled the Silverdome with 75,000 young people?" You know of course, the first thing my team thought was, "Did God tell you that it was gonna be full?" My answer was, "You know what? This is part of our dreams, some of our goals. Just *what if* this is God's will? If it is and God really does want us to be there, what do you think it would take to get there?"

I wasn't saying, "This is God's will." I was asking, "Just *what if* it was? What do you think we would have to do to go in that direction together?" All of a sudden their whole demeanor changed, and so did the conversation: "Well, we could do this or try this. Let's try out this and see if it works." And pretty soon, the whole thing was out of control! It wasn't me pushing, "Come on you guys, I know we can." It was them grabbing hold and saying, "If it is, I think we could try this." Are you following me? The momentum began to come from them instead of me. They rallied around the "What if?" I'm telling you, it has power to get them to buy into the vision. Soon, they'll want to work on the "How."

Talk about the "How." What do I mean by the "How"? There are two "hows." First, "How do we get the vision done right now?" That means next week and next month. The second is broader than that: "How do we get the big plan done?" If you have 10 people in your group today, no matter how hard you work this week, you won't have 1,000 people next week. You won't have 500 next week. You may not even have 100 next week. If you want to get THAT part of the vision, you need to start planning things a year or two in advance. This is the part of the meeting where you will do the strategic planning that will ensure the success of the ministry. You'll divide your planning time between the now visions and the future visions.

Let me give you some tips on how to manage meetings so that these things actually happen.

MANAGING THE MEETING

Establish ground rules. Ground rules make everyone understand up front what you expect of them. They keep people from wasting time, and help maximize the efficiency of your meetings. When people get there, you want them to be there, right? You want them to be focused, not just there in body; you want their minds, their hearts, and their focus too. Let me give you some examples of ground rules that you can use.

- Don't be late.
- Don't interrupt meetings for phone calls unless it's an emergency. Turn off your beepers; turn off your cell phones.
- Don't leave the room once the meeting has started. The point is, once we're here, we're here to stay focused, not to do other things.
- Don't slump in your chair or doodle. These postures indicate lack of interest. Be engaged in the meeting.
- Listen attentively to the contributions of your partners and other people in the room.
- Actively contribute. In Harvard Business School, half of the grade is based on class participation. Forget all the papers and the tests; if you don't contribute during class, you will flunk.
- Focus hard to achieve the group good. It's not about me doing well; it's about everyone doing well.

- Find what's positive and eliminate the negative. Don't simply say, "I don't like that." Find the positive and accentuate that. Then seek to be the kind of participant you expect others to be.

Here's another idea: Don't you hate when people talk about things they've already told you again and again? Then they act like it's the first time anyone ever heard it? Lay the ground rule that anyone may call a time-out: "Time-out. Wait a minute. You've said that before; we've heard that speech." Be careful, people might call a time-out on you. But that's good, because repeating things just wastes people's time.

As the leader, it's your job to run meetings well. If you don't manage them, no one else will.

Define the roles. Make sure you know what your role is as the leader (managing the meeting). Also, help your team leaders be clear on their roles. Sometimes when I'm in a meeting I'll give the marker to someone and say, "Here, you lead this part of the discussion." I want them to be involved and engaged, not just along for the ride, so define the roles within the meeting.

Limit the issues. Don't talk about everything in the world. Choose enough issues to fill up your time and allow enough time for each of them.

Prepare an agenda. Don't just have it in your mind! Write an agenda before you walk in the door.

Be early to your own meetings. I encourage you as a leader to arrive early. This helps with the relationship side of things. "Hey, how are you doing, Sarah?" I'll walk around, rub somebody's shoulder and ask, "What's going on with you?" There's something about touch. Touch shows you care and are involved. You don't have to touch every-body. Just touching two people (in friendly, appropriate ways) creates a positive atmosphere.

Then start on time. It's very important how you begin the meeting. Say, "I'm so glad you're here. We're going to have a great meeting." This is part of depositing value into your leaders. Get announcements out of the way as quickly as possible.

Use the meeting for synergy, not information disper-sal. Minimize announcements. Using meetings to distribute information is a bad use of people's time. If you need to disperse information, send an e-mail beforehand. Many youth pastors use announcements to collect their thoughts, since they're just winging the meeting anyway. On the other hand, you've prepared in advance and have valuable things to actually *discuss* with your team. The value of people is getting them together to think and dialogue.

This goes for your leaders as well. If someone is going to report, have her send you the information ahead of time. Forward it to the group. They can read the information before they get there. Then they can be ready to discuss it when the meeting starts.

At the very beginning, state the objectives and esti-mated time for the meeting. These things need to be clear to all in attendance. If people come in late, don't draw atten-tion to them, just keep going. Make sure that people who come in late or miss a meeting know that it is their

I encourage you as a leader to arrive early. This helps with the relationship side of things.

Having a good team that you love, respect, and enjoy is the best way to accomplish a vision.

responsibility to find out what happened when they weren't there. It is not your responsibility to repeat it all over again to them and be the babysitter.

Periodically, however, restate the meeting objective in order to keep the meeting focused.

Be a moderator, not a partisan. Remain impartial, or at least demonstrate the appearance of impartiality during the meeting. For instance, don't take sides too quickly when people have contradicting opinions. Your value as a leader is to hear all sides on an issue. If you appear to take a side then people will think you're biased, and they will hesitate or hold back from sharing. Stay objective for as long as you can. Try to separate facts from opinions and beliefs.

"I really, really think we should!"

"But why . . . what evidence do you have?"

Watch the pacing of the meeting. Move things along. Don't get so wrapped up in one thing that you run out of time to talk about something important. Be on the lookout for any emotional build-ups. If you know someone gets really passionate about a subject, be ready to try to defuse the discussion if necessary.

Involve everyone. If a team member is sitting there being quiet, don't just let him sit there. Ask, "What do you think, Joe?" Ask his opinion, even though he didn't volunteer any information. He may have a great idea, but you may have to pull it out of him a little bit. Or it might show that he is not prepared, which is good to know too. He'll realize he needs to come prepared next time.

Make people feel important. Affirm people and their contributions. There are two things people on a team need to hear: "That's a great idea," and "You are a valuable part of this team."

Protect the weak. If there are people who don't present strongly in meetings, look out for them. Don't allow others to trample their feelings or ideas. Maybe you need to help them develop in this area, or maybe they don't belong on the team. Either way, you need to protect them.

Be sure to end the meeting. I would encourage you to have a time written down that you will end the meeting. It's your responsibility to keep it from going on forever.

Having a good team that you love, respect, and enjoy is the best way to accomplish a vision. Too many churches, not to mention youth ministries, don't take advantage of team ministry. They may have a board of deacons, and a board of elders, etc., but very few actually work as a team to see a vision come about. Victory is so sweet when you have accomplished it through loving teamwork.

Jesus did this with His disciples. He constantly used team dynamics to pull them together, to give them the vision. He taught them lessons, sent them out, brought them back, then sent them out again. He was pulling them into His vision for the world, and their role in it. That is what you must do if you are going to see your incredible ministry vision from God come to pass.

CHAPTER EIGHT

Preparing for the Rollout

Now that you have completed so much of the work that a real leader does, it is important to "unveil" the vision in a way that draws people in. By now you have had weeks of praying over and thinking through the details of the new vision, but others have not. You are convinced it is God's direction, but they know nothing about it. In order to complete the vision, you must have people agree with your vision, so how you present it to them (the rollout) will either woo them into the vision or drive them away. Remember, we mentioned earlier God's model for leadership: God gives the vision to the leader, and the leader is called to take the people with him.

How you introduce folks to the vision is crucial. It will, in large part, determine whether or not they'll follow.

How you introduce folks to the vision is crucial. It will, in large part, determine whether or not they'll follow. It's as if you're unveiling an amazing sculpture that you've carved in private (of course you have had some of your adult and teen leaders helping you with the plan) for a long time. You want everyone to be thrilled about the new direction. Just telling them, "God has put this on my heart. I know we have only 25 kids in here now, but in a year we can have 200," may not do it.

Part of the rollout is making the dream compelling, but also showing them your plan to accomplish it. This makes the dream believable, and not just a fantasy. They have to know you are serious about the direction and that you have done the homework. Some people get so excited about an idea they have for ministry that they talk about it prematurely, and as a result it comes off as a whim. When they see the planning that you and your team have put into it in advance, they will know you are serious about pursuing the dream. Our job as Youth Specialists is to not only give them the dream, but give them a glimpse of how it will happen.

In this chapter, we'll deal with these things that come *before* the actual rollout. Then, in the chapter to come, we'll cover a few important principles to guide you through the period *after* the rollout.

GETTING YOUR DUCKS IN A ROW

What things must you do before your big event? Here

are eight things I've found absolutely essential for rollout success:

1. Don't go past . . . your pastor. As Youth Specialists in a church, part of our challenge is to help our pastors understand what God is burning into our hearts—and show that it is lining up with the broader vision of the church. Make sure the pastor is fully on board, because if it is a vision that is going to rock your region, a dream that will really change the community, then you must gather plenty of support.

At all costs, avoid having your pastor find out about things accidentally, through other people. Instead, woo your pastor. Don't just walk in and say, "This is what God is telling us. Obey or perish!"

Instead, very early on in the dreaming process, try something like this: "Pastor, the Lord has really been putting some things inside of me about the direction for the youth for the next year or so. I just want to make sure it lines up with where your heart is for the young people in this church. So maybe I could just share a couple of things with you and see what you think about these ideas."

Then . . . share those ideas.

Of course, some pastors will resist. You then need to back up a little further and help him develop a heart before you share your plan.

How can you do that? You might say things like: "Pastor, I've done some research about the kids in our high

As Youth Specialists in a church, part of our challenge is to help our pastors understand what God is burning into our hearts—and show that it is lining up with the broader vision of the church.

Most pastors will want to help these kids.
We just need to personalize the need
and help them understand that it is
all taking place right here
in our community.

school and this is what I've found . . ." Then tell what you know. It's already broken your own heart to know these things—the abuse, the loneliness, the drug use, the abortion, the sexual experimentation and disease. Who could know these things and not be moved to action? Yet be gentle, submissive, and—above all—exercise patience. You might say something like: "What do you think, Pastor; do you think we should do anything to help these kids in our community?"

Most pastors will want to help these kids. We just need to personalize the need and help them understand that it is all taking place *right here in our community.* "Pastor, maybe we can do some things to help these kids." He then will begin to ask whether you have any ideas . . .

2. Ramp up your teen leaders and adult volunteers. Far in advance, pull some teens in that demonstrate leadership and tell them that God is burning things into your heart. Ask them whether they want to help. Then, when you have your rollout, you'll already have plenty of teens who are excited and behind you—even encouraging others. Pull them into the dream before telling everyone else. You may also get good ideas from these teens. (Note: Don't go to them for ideas about where they think the ministry should go; that is your job as the leader. But you *can* say, "This is where God is taking us, so do you guys have any ideas on how we should get there?" And don't offer any voting control. Just let them give you ideas and then you pray and choose.) You will want to already have assigned them different areas in your flow chart so that organization is in place to accomplish the dream before you roll it out.

Look now at your CD-ROM again. The first page of the file titled "Rollout," asks you to do some thinking about key people who will come alongside you and help as you reveal the new direction of your youth ministry. Ask God to show you people with ideas and enthusiasm! The second page helps you prepare for the rollout event itself.

3. Don't start until . . . you're finished planning. Okay, let's back up a minute. Don't forget that there's a difference between *having* a plan and *implementing* the plan. Often people start dreaming about all they're going to do for God, and they get so excited about it that they *start implementing it before the planning is complete.* "Oh, we're going to do this and this and this!" They talk to people before they've thought the whole thing through.

What happens then? A couple of months later you are

Don't forget that there's a difference between having a plan and implementing the plan.

still putting the plan together and still "sort of" talking about it—with a lot less energy. Naturally, this causes people to lose confidence in your plan and think that you are just a talker, not a doer. Do not start talking about the plan (to the group) or implementing any part of a plan until the planning is complete—until you really do know where you *are* and where you're *going* and exactly *how* you are going to get there.

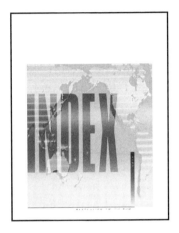

When you first begin to pull the plan together, it will be a little fuzzy, like an artist's first blotches of paint on a canvas. Who can tell what it will become? But she keeps coming back to it, and eventually we see something clearly take shape. With the final touches, everything is crystal clear. *That's* when it's time to start showing it around.

In the Index of your CD-ROM, you will find several letters and organizational tools that may help you as you roll out your youth ministry plan. Feel free to reproduce or adapt them for your own use.

4. Believe, and make the plan . . . believable. Now you have the plan, the step-by-step process, all laid out in charts with a mission statement, objectives, goals, core values—the whole nine yards. Your next job is to make the vision believable to the kids and to the leaders and parents. You must instill confidence. But here's the key concept I want you to remember:

> *Others may not believe in the plan, but they believe that you believe it will work.*

They see that you believe the plan so much—with so

much passion and practical sweat-and-tears commitment—that they are enabled to believe it too. Clearly, you have to believe that the dream is from God. Then it's simple: you pour your heart out.

Whenever a giant new step is taken in ministry, people need to know that the leader really believes this is from God. When we were preparing to move our ministry headquarters to Texas, the numbers all lined up, but my board of directors asked, "Do you believe this is the Lord's direction?" They didn't care if it was logical—if it wasn't God's direction. My leadership team, who would have to move their families if they were to stay in Teen Mania, had to have great faith. Finally I told them, "I have so much faith this is from God, that even if you don't, I have enough faith for all of you!" Based on that, they all sold their houses and moved their families and followed the dream!

5. Tease your teens. Part of a great rollout is creating anticipation in the youth group about what's coming. Make some off-the-cuff statements like, "God has been putting some great things in my heart about where we are going as a ministry . . . oh, I can't talk to you about that now . . . I will tell you more later." Then at another time you say something like, "Oh, guys, I am so excited about where God is going to take us—oh sorry, I can't really talk about that now." Then later you can say, "On this date, everything is going to change. God is stirring me up, and I can't wait to tell you everything. On May 15 (or whatever date) I will . . ."

A couple of weeks later, tease them again, while you are still several months in advance of the rollout. Be clear about this, though: you're not throwing pieces of the vision out there. You are simply building a sense of anticipation. A week before the rollout, that anticipation will include a lot of detail.

If you do this right, it should be a launching pad for your dream. For example, one week before rollout, you could hold a funeral service for your old youth group. Do it right—play a CD with organ music, have a real coffin, wear black. Don't even announce it; just let kids come in and tell them you are burying the old youth group. "Here lie all the old attitudes, the old names, the old program, everything we have done. We are going to bury it all and only take with us what God wants us to take." Write all those "old, dead things" down and throw them in the coffin. Then offer your eulogy: "We are gathered here today in remembrance of . . ." Finally, have someone carry the coffin out and invite the teens to say their final goodbyes.

Kids won't know what to expect for next week, will they? But they'll know it will be new. The old is buried! At the end of the funeral service, tell them to get ready for the resurrection, the revelation of the new dream, the vision of "where God is taking us." Leave them with a sense of anticipation—a whole new picture of how their future will look.

If this sounds like a fun idea to you, go to your CD-ROM and open the file titled "Change." The first page will

help you get started as you plan for a "funeral service" for the old ways of doing youth group.

Tease the parents, too. Ask your senior pastor to include several announcements in the Sunday bulletin. Write little teasers that say, "God is taking our young people somewhere new. We are gearing up to do something incredible. It will be awesome, so get ready for the rollout." Prime the parents, so that when you're ready to unroll the vision to them, they'll more readily support it.

6. Preparing to make a BIG DEAL! You already know you're going to have a youth group name, logo, and room ready to unveil. Remember that your kids really do need their own identity. That is why schools have mascots. Here are some things you can do with these identifiers to make a splash:

- Develop your own unique logo and get a banner made . . . BIG; have it ready and up on the wall, covered.
- Make T-shirts with your logo and Bible verse.
- Have business cards proclaiming what you are all about, so you and the teens can pass them out to all their friends. You could make them look like a ticket—"Free Admission to next Wednesday!" Be sure to include the new name of your youth group, your logo, and mission statement.
- Make a brochure showing "where we are now, and where we will be going over the next six months to a year."

With these small but effective actions, people begin to realize that they're not just coming to "a youth something." They are heading into a vision. When you give them a big and broad vision, they'll want to be a part of it.

7. Paint the picture . . . for picture-perfect impact. Before the rollout, think about how you will use your words to paint a multicolored, multifaceted picture in their minds. Your youth room may not be the coolest yet, but there should be a clear difference between what it looked like last week and what it looks like this week. Don't just ask, "Here it is; who likes it?" Do an actual unveiling. Have the logo, mission statement, goals for the year, picture of the youth room, etc. all covered up, so when the kids walk in they

Make the vision so compelling that it fills in all the blanks between the dots of your plan.

know something is there but can't tell what it is. Then bring people all together for the big revelation. This is what you are doing with your vision, very slowly and deliberately getting ready to unveil it.

One thing you might want to do is prepare a video or a Power-Point presentation. Part of the unveiling is to say, "Here is the vision, and let me show you how we are going to get there." This is the time to connect the dots for everyone involved. Display the plan—three months, six months, nine months, one year. Show them what the flowchart looks like, and convey with passion how each person will be a part of this thing God is doing among you.

I can just hear you painting the picture, even now: "When people walk in these doors, they're going to feel so much love and acceptance. And we will have all kinds of kids here—some with tattoos and weird hair and piercings. They will all come. Be ready to open up your arms and hug them!"

How are we going to get 200 kids coming in the door? "We're going to have a happening service! So when they all get here, they'll enjoy an amazing band and riveting video clips. There's going to be drama, and comedy, and you will be putting those things together! Listen—you will reach your own generation for Jesus! *Can you think of anything more awesome than that?"*

Make the vision so compelling that it fills in all the blanks between the dots of your plan. Spell it out clearly to them. I would encourage you to have a couple of your leaders, adults and teens that you've pulled aside earlier, prepared to speak. (But make them promise secrecy until the unveiling night.) That night, call them up and have them offer testimonies. Let them share from their own hearts: "We can do this, I *know* we can . . ."

You have now laid it out. Now the rubber meets the road.

8. Ask people to commit to the Dream. After you've spent time painting the vision, you begin to ask the question, "Who is in this with me?" It's a simple question you can ask in many different ways, but at some point you'll need to say something like, "You guys can come here and attend, no problem. But, from this point on, *if you are going to be a member, then you need to get involved in the vision.*"

Coaches do this when they plan for their championship seasons. It causes every player to make significant, sacrificial changes in lifestyle and priorities. They get up early, work hard in the weight room, eat right, and kiss that pavement every day. They know that they will endure pain. But, because of the vision, they *want* to do it.

You can do the same thing: "This is where we are going; are you with me? I need to know you are with me— and it means that you get enlisted in the plan in some way. You may be a greeter or you may help put things in the mail." Since you need all of your jobs lined up in advance, you begin asking the question at the strategic time. Follow through with those who are ready to get plugged into this vision by saying, "I need your time and I need your energy to see this happen." Tell them, "If we harness this energy together, then we can do this thing. But I need to know who will be with me."

Go ahead, draw a line in the sand; have an altar call. Who will be part of this vision that has come from God? "God is going to use you, not just me. All of us together!" Present such a compelling dream that it is worth the pain and sweat.

Have people come down to the front, and let them

CHURCH ON THE BIG SCREEN

We have rolled out the steps used in [*Double Vision*]. We did the big reveal on a Sunday during our first youth-led worship service. A lot of people were amazed. I also used a lot of . . . stats and made a video to show the church on the big screen we installed in the youth center. Big hit!

—Duke, Youth Specialist

know, in great detail, the commitment you will ask of them—the hours in the office, for example. Lay it all out, because those who are grasped by the vision will be inspired to work harder than they've ever worked before. Because you have a detailed flowchart for your operational plan, you already know how many people you need, and where you need them. Enlist them that night.

Once you have prayed at the front of the auditorium or church, show them on the flow-chart the different areas that will forward the vision. Have each of the different area leaders at the back of the room. Describe each area and who is in charge. Then dismiss your teens to go to the area that interests them. That's part of the package. Everyone gets involved that night in some part of the vision. Give them the business cards, T-shirts, etc., as a

sign that you know they are committed. Once they're in their respective areas, make sure each leader is prepared to tell them what he needs for them to do, when the next meeting is, and then pray over that area.

That night, all things change. Get them plugged in that night.

Finally, remember that this will be a big deal only if the parents are fully with you. Maybe in the past you've had to beg your parents to bring their kids to a youth meeting. No more! Now that you've told your youth, you can reveal the vision to their parents.

Go back to your computer and look at page two of the CD-ROM file titled "Change." Keep a running list of people who are supporting you in the vision.

To see revolution in this generation, we need a lot more than youth pastors caring about kids. We need every adult who calls himself a Christian to care about kids. When MTV wants to reach a generation, they don't just hire one person; they hire an army of people. Everybody at MTV cares about reaching teenagers with a corrupt message. We need an army of adults who care about church, and we need the whole church to care about your youth and to pray for the vision. You may want to sign up your parents, pastors, and deacons to go through the *Battle Cry for a Generation* book and study guide. You don't want to be alone in this effort to double your youth group every year for the next five years. We need our churches to be like hospitals to the broken-hearted teens of this generation!

This rollout is the night when all your planning begins to reap fruit. Your dream will start to become what you have seen in your heart for a long time.

CHAPTER NINE

The Ongoing Role of the Youth Specialist

If you've come this far in the book, you might be tempted to think, "Wow! Now I'm going to be really busy!" There are youth worker conferences you'll need to attend to help you discover a million things that you could try. The catalogs that fill your mailbox every day with new ideas and products will need immediate investigating. Right? Wrong!

Now that your plan is in place (and assuming you have unveiled it correctly), and your adult and teen leaders are leading the charge to accomplish the vision, you must decide where *you* should use *your* energy, based on your dream that the Lord has given you for youth ministry.

How is it that a CEO with 40,000 employees can run a

It's important to remember that the reason you have leaders is so they can do the job, not you.

company with time to spare, yet many youth leaders hardly have time to breathe? CEOs spend their time differently than you do. They invest their time and energy doing *only* the tasks no one else can do.

As Youth Specialists, we must keep asking ourselves, "What are the tasks *only* I can do?" Decide what tasks can be handled well by someone else, and let them go for it! After you have rolled out the vision for your youth ministry, you must focus your energy doing eight things that no one else can do:

1. Keep managing the plan. Take a close look at every one of your leaders' weekly reports and make sure they are "on plan." You know the old saying, "People don't do what you expect; they do what you inspect." It's true! As you look at their reports, which we described earlier, always respond with your comments. E-mail is a great way to communicate—it's fast and easy. I suggest you e-mail good comments only; if you need to correct, always do it in person. Your team needs to know that you are watching what they do, and whether or not they are moving in the right direction. You will spend time coaching them in any area where they are falling short.

It's important to remember that the reason you have leaders is so they can do the job, not you. Keep pushing them and developing them so they will be successful at their tasks. Just because you are inspecting what they are doing does not mean that you should start doing it yourself. Be careful to avoid this temptation.

2. Keep preparing a service each week. This includes all the elements of keeping teens' attention and helping them to really engage in their relationship with the Lord. Using media, PowerPoint, movie clips, object lessons, and discussion guides can all be a part of a creative, interactive service that really connects with their hearts. Obviously it means you must be prepared to speak and deliver great content.

If you have never taken any speaking courses, and you've never read anything that will help develop your speaking ability, begin now! If kids are bringing their friends to Wednesday nights, make sure what you do throughout the service is going to make those teens want to come back!

For the kids who already passionately love God, make sure you have a steak to put on the table for them. Too often I've seen kids get on fire at camp or at an Acquire the Fire weekend, or a mission trip, and they come back to sit in the front row and be fed. But the youth leader is talking to everyone else! "You guys need to get on fire," he says. And the kids in the front are saying "Amen!" Then the leader says, "You guys in the back need to be like these guys in the front." This goes on for two months, and all the kids start to think: "Haven't we heard all this before?" The fire goes out. They start thinking they've heard everything in the Bible, because the same single message is repeated over and over again. Don't let that happen!

If you don't feed the kids spiritually, they'll get bored and distracted. The world will get their attention and the next thing you know you'll hear of them involved in some sin and lament, "I guess they were not as committed as I thought they were." Yes they were; they just starved to death spiritually even though they were coming to church! A Youth Specialist would never let this happen. We must specialize in making these on-fire converts into solid warriors and disciples!

Kids will starve to death spiritually if we do not feed them.

Kids will starve to death spiritually if we do not feed them. At the most basic level, this means you can't be trying to think of something to say while driving to the meeting! It is our solemn responsibility to make sure each of our messages to the kids is awesome and amazing. When kids leave your Wednesday night service, they should walk away thinking, "This is the best ministry in the whole world!" They should be convinced in their hearts that nothing could possibly be more important than coming back next week because, "I love it here, I get fed, I feel loved here, and I feel God's presence here." Each week, make sure all the elements of an amazing meeting are in place and do it with excellence.

As you're planning your weekly meeting, make sure that your teaching themes are geared around your dream. For example, if a big part of your dream is to develop kids who love to worship God, then take three or four weeks to talk about "how to become a worship animal." That is what you want them to become. And if a big part of your vision also includes helping the kids become "ministry monsters," take a month and dwell on that. If part of your thing is about missions, spend weeks on it. As you teach, give awesome examples, make it funny, interactive, heartfelt, and inspiring. God may change your plan from time to time if something is really brewing in your heart, or some emergency comes up in your community. But you can keep coming back to the dream that drives the agenda of your meeting topics. *Your service topics ought to be driven by your vision.*

3. Keep rolling out the dream to the whole church body. Once you unveil the vision and plan to the pastor and the kids, you need to follow with the entire church body. Why? Because you need every member behind you.

Obviously, you need parents praying for you. You want them saying, "Amen! Amen!" to your inspiring declaration of the plan. "Folks, Pastor Jones bought into this thing, and I am telling you I need every adult to be praying for us and considering becoming a volunteer. Pray, please pray!" You want them to take ownership of the vision.

Enlist their hearts by constantly giving them stories about real-life teens in your church and community. Show them the hurting teens, the successful teens, the failing teens. Appeal to their compassion, because church people have good hearts, but they need to see and feel what you are talking about.

Then, when these folks see young people coming in with weird hair and piercings, they too are ready to hug them and love them and be the "parents" these kids don't have at home. Some of your church members, whose hearts have been melted for young people, will begin to take kids under their wings. Our job is to give our adults a vision of what they *could* do because most do not know what they *can* do. This is not a burden to us; this is part of our job!

The bottom line is, many adults are afraid of young people. So we can hug the "scary" kids in front of them. (Wouldn't it be great if every visitor who came into our meetings got hugged 10 times?) Suppose we gave church members such a vision that, when they're at the checkout counter with the kid who bags their groceries, they say, "You've gotta come to our youth meetings at church; they're terrific!" Wouldn't that be awesome?

You can keep coming back to the dream that drives the agenda of your meeting topics.

Our job is to give our adults a vision of what they could do because most do not know what they can do.

Give the church a vision. Keep finding ways to keep it in front of them and keep every heart involved.

4. *Keep looking at the forest.* Keep the big picture before you at all times. Yes, it's easy to become sidetracked by problems, fires to extinguish, and conflicts to resolve. Nevertheless, you must take your eyes off the individual trees and stand back to survey the whole forest. It's your job to keep a finger on the pulse of the whole living body of ministry, so you know if all the parts are working together to fulfill the plan—or not. You don't get down and micromanage each part. But you do poke your head in on different parts of the ministry you created and see if everyone is okay—encouraging, reminding, and lifting them up as needed: "Listen, I've got a Scripture for you guys," or, "Man, that looks great; good job!" Ask questions that refer the team back to the big plan:

- Are we on track?
- How is the worship team doing?
- Are you guys coming together in the media committee?
- How's it coming with transportation?
- What's happening these days with drama planning?
- Is everything that we prepared and planned happening, or not?

Maybe you're thinking, "Ron, if I have to keep my eyes on the big picture, does that mean I can never counsel kids one-on-one again?" No. What it means is that you're raising up other leaders who can do things like that. Sadly, some of us feel that we're called to be friends with every one of our kids. But if we have a hundred kids in our group, it's impossible for us to be friends with every one.

You say, "But that sounds so cold!" Keep this in mind: we're called to be *leaders* to them, all of them. More than our friendship, the kids need our God-given ability to teach them how to be strong men and women of God. That's what they need.

Yes, some kids may think that you preach really well on Wednesday nights and if they hung out with you as your friend, they would get more of that. And they probably would get more of that—but you can't do it with 100 teens! So you commission your leadership group of teen leaders and adult leaders to be friends to all the others. They can counsel. They can take calls from kids late at night, asking for prayer because parents are fighting. You take the higher-level emergency calls, because *you have to look over the whole forest.* You have the whole dream to manage, a sacred stewardship from the Lord. You can't afford to get lost in the trees.

5. Keep feeding your teen leaders and adult volunteers. You need an army of adults to work with you. You need an army of teenage young people to work with you. Therefore, part of your job is to know how to enlist them effectively.

You must take your eyes off the individual trees and stand back to survey the whole forest.

You have the whole dream to manage, a sacred stewardship from the Lord. You can't afford to get lost in the trees.

Don't ask people to give you anything (their time, their labor, their love, etc.) *without giving them something in return.*

What do you give back? You give spiritual food, piled high with tons of encouragement. Your team meetings should be so much more than simply handing out assignments. Instead, ask yourself: "What am I going to do to plant a seed into their lives? What am I going to do to build my team up? What am going to do to make them stronger men and women of God?" Why? Part of your vision is to take this army of teens and make them into robust leaders. So you will do the research, read the books, and listen to the tapes to figure out what's going to make them into great leaders. As a result, you come into every meeting with that agenda.

Keep feeding your team; don't let them go dry on you. It is easy to overlook them because they are already strong, but make sure you keep feeding them, too!

6. Keep raising money. Sorry, but you can't quit doing this. And don't feel ripped off; it's part of life. That doesn't mean you should be taking M&Ms everywhere, selling them door-to-door all by yourself. But do realize that you simply must use some of your time for this.

Every nonprofit organization has to raise money. But take heart. If your ministry is really going to touch lives and change hearts, then it's worth it. On your agenda must be, "How, exactly, am I going to fund this thing?"

Yes, we now have a wonderful youth center. But a month later, will the doors be closed? Yes, if you're not

Keep feeding your team; don't let them go dry on you.

bringing in the funds to support it. If everything revolves around getting the thing started—rather than thinking the thing through and keeping the doors open—then failure looms.

Some youth leaders are shortsighted and say, "God will supply somehow; let's just get the doors open!" But my experience is that *fulfilling our God-given responsibilities is a part of the blessing God graciously gives us.* Therefore, a big part of our job is to think long term. If you need proof, consider: How many empty youth buildings dot the country at the moment? How many coffee houses were started by a ministry, funded for a month or two, and then the doors slammed shut?

Money. It's part of our job, not a curse. The great thing is that if people can get money to fund stupid causes—to save the worms, to cool down the planet—surely we can get money for the greatest cause of all—reaching a young generation for Jesus before He returns.

7. Keep reiterating the vision. Make the vision fresh, real, and alive every day—every time you preach, or teach, or talk. The Lord of the universe is hardly boring! We can follow Him, constantly conveying the awesome adventure

If everything revolves around getting the thing started—rather than thinking the thing through and keeping the doors open—then failure looms.

Money. It's part of our job,
not a curse.

of involvement in His dreams for us. More stories, more new statistics about youth, more current events, more high-school stories in the news—all of this from you—help teens to continue on and press into the vision.

We tend to think that if we say it one time that they get it. They don't. Constantly look into how you can make the dream compelling and clear to them. Say it a hundred times, because they didn't get it completely or as clearly as you got it. You must sell the vision . . . and resell it.

8. Keep developing yourself. We must keep growing ourselves as leaders, as women and men of God. This means finding people who are beyond us in spiritual maturity and/or leadership skill to mentor us. It means asking, "What can I learn from them?" whether it's people that we meet one-on-one in our church, or our pastor, or leaders in our community, or authors of the books that we read. It's

our job to learn from them and grow better, stronger, and more competent.

It is your responsibility to let God grow you as a leader of teens. If you don't keep growing, you won't be able to take anyone else with you. While you lay out your dream, introduce it, unveil it, and get the kids committed and involved, you must keep taking in what you need—so you can keep giving out what you've received.

As you build your youth ministry from the ground up, you can't and shouldn't do everything yourself. But you must do these eight things to continue to watch the dream unfold in front of you. It does take focus. It does take work. But you can do it! In fact, you *must* do it. Your call is to rescue a generation of young people and speak truth into their lives.

Before you go on to the next chapter, take some time to think about the eight things youth leaders must focus their time on. Go to your computer now and open the CD-ROM file "Change" and look at pages three and four. Focus your energy on these things that no one else can do but you!

While you lay out your dream, introduce it, unveil it, and get the kids committed and involved, you must keep taking in what you need—so you can keep giving out what you've received.

CHAPTER TEN

Preempting Problems as You Grow

Problems. Conflicts. Messy messes! We all have them in ministry, and we all want to move through them as quickly as possible. The good news, of course, is that most of our significant problems result from growth. And growth is good, bringing much blessing to everyone involved. We get to minister to more kids, we get to touch more lives, and we get to see more people coming to Christ. We also face many more sticky difficulties.

But is it possible to prevent some of the problems in the first place? Yes! In this chapter we'll look at some growth-related problems you can expect, and I'll describe a few proactive actions you can take.

Sadly, some folks who work with youth apply a

We must not settle for becoming a wide river; we want to be a deep river.

ministry-devastating logic: "Well, the more kids there are, the more problems there are. That means I must stay small and minister to fewer kids—see fewer kids come to Christ—because I don't want more problems."

No, we simply need to grow wiser so we can minister to more. Anticipate problems so you can resolve them. Nip potential problems in the bud by asking yourself a few pointed questions . . .

Is my heart deepening along with my ministry growth? As I mentioned in the previous chapter, your heart for God must grow right along with your ministry. It's also your responsibility to make sure that your leadership skills grow, that your family is stable, and that your personal life stays wholesome.

When our ministry expands, it's so exciting! As it grows wider and broader, so do we, until suddenly . . . we go shallow. We must not settle for becoming a *wide* river; we want to be a *deep* river. The danger for youth leaders is that as we seek to *expand* the ministry, we may sacrifice *depth* . . . our own! What good is it if we are full of one-line zingers that can really inspire an audience if we, ourselves, are shallow?

Let's be diligent about being in the Word and in prayer. Let's commit to challenging ourselves and letting our spouses and others speak truth into our lives. We must make every effort as the ministry expands, to continue on a deepening journey, growing along with our ministry. There is nothing worse than a shallow person, out of touch with God, trying to lead a growing ministry.

Am I remembering who I truly am? Monitor your ego! So you once had 30 kids, and now you have 60 kids. All of a sudden you have become an expert, and everybody in town is saying, "Wow! Did you hear they have their own bus, and their own youth building? This guy must know what he's doing!"

Naturally, you start thinking, "Hey, I'm doing pretty well." You didn't mean to develop this attitude, but it sneaks in. "I smell pretty good, I look pretty good, and, you know, I guess I *am* the coolest youth pastor in these parts." You may never consciously say it; you just start acting like it. Here's a good biblical corrective:

> *For by the grace given me I say to every one of you: Do not think of yourself more highly than you ought, but rather think of yourself with sober judgment, in accordance with the measure of faith God has given you.*
> —Romans 12:3

As your ministry begins to grow, God begins to bless. God does it. It is *His* work, *His* Kingdom, *His* glory.

And who are we? Well, we are sons and daughters of the Most High God. We are not God, though. We are sons and daughters of the Most High, joint heirs with Jesus Christ. But we are not Jesus Christ. We have to know this, deep inside, so we can lean on the One who is our life and our strength and our reason for being. Everything flows from Him and works for His glory. Not our glory.

"But Ron," some say, "I have such a struggle staying humble!" Here's a great way to do it: have great quiet times. It is quite difficult to stay arrogant when you go face-to-face with God every day—when you bow your knee and your heart before Jesus regularly.

Can you worship the Lord of all with all of your heart, all by yourself? If so, can you feel proud in His presence? Or

When your ministry expands, and you feel the subtle pull of an expanding ego, spend some time in quietness before God.

is it simply *gratitude* that wells up? (What else could there be?)

When your ministry expands, and you feel the subtle pull of an expanding ego, spend some time in quietness before God. Ask yourself: "Have I forgotten who God is, and who I am?" Then it's easy to keep yourself in perspective.

How proactive am I with my pastor? You've got your pastor "on board," of course, and he wants everything to work as you've planned. But here's what can happen: if your youth ministry really begins to grow, then people will start paying attention to . . . *you.* That's fine, but . . .

> . . . *you don't ever want the pastor to think that you are "doing your own thing."*
> . . . *you don't ever want the pastor to think that you believe, "This is my church."*
> . . . *you don't ever want the pastor to think that you have no need for spiritual authority in the church.*

You want your pastor to know that you are in total submission to him and to the church. In fact, this is the spirit of a leader that Jesus held up as an example for the kingdom.

> *When Jesus had entered Capernaum, a centurion came to him, asking for help. "Lord," he said, "my servant lies at home paralyzed and in terrible suffering."*
> *Jesus said to him, "I will go and heal him."*

The centurion replied, "Lord, I do not deserve to have you come under my roof. But just say the word, and my servant will be healed. For I myself am a man under authority, with soldiers under me. I tell this one, 'Go,' and he goes; and that one, 'Come,' and he comes. I say to my servant, 'Do this,' and he does it."

When Jesus heard this, he was astonished and said to those following him, "I tell you the truth, I have not found anyone in Israel with such great faith."

—Matthew 8:5–10

This centurion held authority *over* scores of soldiers. Though he was a commander, he started by saying, "I am a man *under* authority." So it should be with us as we talk to our pastors. We can constantly remind him and ourselves that, "I am under your authority. I am under your leadership. Do you feel good about this plan . . . this event . . . this outreach, Pastor? What do you think about this idea?" We can submit things on a regular basis so that there is never a sense of "that youth guy taking over."

Instead, be proactive. Constantly, regularly, take the initiative to remind your senior pastor, "I am under your authority here. If this thing grows it is because you are blessing it, and you are allowing it to happen. It is all still under your leadership." Be the one to bring it up, so the pastor never has to say to you, "Remember, you are still under the authority of this church." No, you should be reminding him, "I am a part of your ministry here. This is awesome what God is doing. I am just a small part of it."

To what extent am I caring for individuals? Never forget that ministry is about people. It's not about how well we run a meeting, how well we preach, how well we administrate. It's about caring for people—talking to them, listening to them, encouraging them at every turn.

If there is no true caring, people start wondering, "Wait

Never forget that ministry is about people.

a minute; is this just a big show? Is this merely an organiza-tion or is this a *ministry?*" On the other hand, if teens and adults know that you care about them, that you really love them, then you don't have to remind them by saying, "We really care about people around here!" They already *know* you care about them because they see it and feel it.

> *When a king sits on his throne to judge, he winnows out all evil with his eyes.*
> —Proverbs 20:8

If you want to make sure your ministry is not "over-thrown," then make sure the people you lead know that you love them. Stay connected to them, talk to them, and listen to them. Before any big event, I'm usually out just walking through the auditorium, talking to kids, trying to stay con-nected, listening, caring, praying with some of them. Maybe you can't talk to everybody, but you can at least communi-cate care for those you do meet.

When they know that they are loved, you won't have to worry about people you serve in your authority. You pre-empt problems.

As my ministry grows, am I becoming more and more a statesman? This simply means that all the other youth groups in your area *will start looking to you* as your ministry grows. People from far and wide will call, "Hey, I heard your youth group has doubled in the last few months. How did you do that? Can I come visit sometime? Can you come and tell me about it or visit with our leaders?"

These folks are often really struggling and hurting.

They'll ask you to pray for them and encourage them. They'll seek your guidance and even your companionship.

What can you do? Realize that an element of statesmanship must come with your success. As the Bible says: "A generous man will prosper; he who refreshes others will himself be refreshed" (Prov. 11:25). As God blesses us with success and growth, we're called to refresh others. Yes, give away the tips you have learned. Explain how to minister, how to grow a ministry, how to do this and that. Give it away and you bless others, helping them grow.

Youth groups aren't in competition! There are a lot more kids than all of us can handle right now. I know it's "not your job description," but give anyway. God will bless you as you refresh others.

This is a good time to think about preempting problems in more depth. Go to your computer and open your CD-ROM to the file titled "Problems." The first page will help you evaluate the steps you must take to remain a proactive leader. Be as specific as you possibly can.

Am I constantly grooming my leaders so they can lead autonomously? As a ministry grows, some leaders will be tempted to stay involved in the same way—doing everything. Instead, we need to work ourselves out of a lot of jobs. We do that with leadership training and delegation. It avoids all kinds of problems.

God will bless you as you refresh others.

1. The ministry's quality. You are constantly involved in evaluating: "Is this good ministry, was that a good altar call, is this good worship?" You must monitor such things all the time. You don't have to do it all, but you set the standard.

2. The ministry's vision and direction. You can't say, "It's Brother Bob's job to lead the direction." No, if you are the leader, that is your job.

3. The ministry's finances. You have to be directly involved with funding. You can't say, "But I just want to think about the ministry." People will start to spend money in all kinds of foolish ways—or money won't come in at all. So many ministries cease to exist—or leaders get kicked out of ministry—because something bogus happened with the dollars. Don't let this happen to you.

This is the sticky part: delegate even things that you *could* do (and that you could do very well). Groom other people to do those things. Then you can focus on those things that *only you can do*, the things you are *supposed* to do.

Take worship, for example. You help the leader understand: "This is the kind of worship I want, this is how many songs I want, this is how intense I want it to be, this is the kind of band or worship team I want you to have, and this is the way I want the kids to participate." You are shaping, molding, and defining. As you convey these principles to your leaders, soon they can proceed without you having to operate for them. You can back away, just as Jesus did.

Remember that Jesus had the disciples constantly watching Him work. In time His trainees were allowed to do some of it: "Hey, could you pray for that woman over there?" "Could you lay your hands on this one, or put some mud on that man?" Eventually He said, "Okay, I'm going to be in the background, but My Spirit will be with you. So now you go out and do all these things in My name. Be My eyes and hands and feet. Show the love and skill that I conveyed to you, and then come back to tell Me how it went."

He let them do it, and so must we.

With Acquire the Fire, I have a great team of staff and interns who operate things. I can show up at ten minutes before seven on a Friday night, walk on the stage, and everything is set. I know that, not only is all the technical stuff done, but people are prayed up, people are focused, and people are ready to minister. It just happens.

It is the same with the mission trips we do in the summers. For a long time I used to travel to the countries to investigate them before we went. Then I would come back and do logistics and take care of all the details. Eventually, though, I worked myself out of this job. I took some people with me to those countries and taught them how to set things up. Now I'm involved in choosing some of the countries, but other qualified leaders set up all the logistics and handle every detail of a massive trip. I simply show up for the training when we all come together on our campus in Garden Valley. The point is, delegate or die young. (Or maybe you'll just be delirious your entire life!)

Look now at page two of the CD-ROM file "Problems." As you answer the questions on the page, think about how best to develop your leaders.

Developing Your Leaders

We need to understand what to delegate and what things not to delegate.

Having said all this about delegation, I must warn you: some things can't be delegated. There are still some areas of the ministry in which I am very much involved. You see, we need to understand what to delegate and what things not to delegate. At least three things should never be handled by others alone:

Am I refining ministry more than doing ministry? Once you have everything up and running, you'll spend your time going from one department to another, refining the picture. It's as if you are "tasting" the flavor of the whole ministry to see what needs to be added or taken away: "How does this part of the ministry taste?"

Let's say you find out that the evangelism team is going out every week, and they are only getting one person saved. So you go to that department to "taste" it— to see if that part of the ministry really agrees with your heart. You spend some time working with your evangelism leader, tweaking and refining how things work there.

Maybe you sense that the worship time was a little too long or boring or a little bit too much hype, not really intimate with God. You spend some time working on that with the worship leaders. When you are finished there, you move on to another area and spend some time with those leaders. "Does this taste right? How does this line up with what is in my heart?"

You're not doing all the ministry work anymore. You can now rotate to different parts of the ministry, tasting here, tasting there. If anything doesn't taste right, you mix in new ingredients until it's right.

Go to your computer again, and refer back to the same file, "Problems." Answer the questions on the page about "Developing Your Leaders." Remember, your job is not to do everything. It's just to make sure all the jobs line up with what is in your heart, and to empower your leaders to lead.

Am I staying spiritually connected to my kids? The Bible says in Proverbs 27:23: "Know the condition of your flocks." We are shepherds, and we do have precious sheep. Do we know their condition? Which of the kids are hurting; which are in spiritual trouble?

Here's one thing to know about teenagers: they are experts at being teenagers. They know what is cool. So if you keep asking them questions, you too will become more and more of an expert on teenagers.

One of the things we do to stay connected with kids is to work with them on our video scripts. We run them by the young people. Kids tweak them, tear them apart, chew them up, and spit them out. And then we *rewrite* the scripts. We run the rewrites by them, and then we do it again, and again, and again. We make sure we are not a bunch of old people saying, "This is really cool!"

I really have no idea what is cool. (How can any of us? It changes all the time.) Let's say you have an idea for a drama you want to do. Don't just say, "Oh, this is really awesome," when they are saying, "Oh great, I don't want to bring my friends to this." Why not run it by the young people?

Staying connected to kids will help you develop a quality program that attracts young people and ministers to them where

Staying connected to kids will help you develop a quality program that attracts young people and ministers to them where they are.

they are. Teens are the experts on how they think and how their friends think.

I hope these questions will help you identify and prevent some of the common problems that occur in a growing ministry. As you grow and resolve each challenge, be ready to offer praise and thanks to the Lord. It is He who motivates you and creates every good thing that appens as you exercise your gifts for His glory.

Go to your CD-ROM again and find the file titled "10 Must Haves." On this inventory, you can rate yourself on the 10 essential areas for success in youth ministry. As you build your ministry and implement the strategies outlined in this book, you will find that you make great improvements in each of these areas. Come back to the inventory in six months and see the gains. Take it now and again to monitor your progress as you become a Youth Specialist!

Now, get ready to dig into the last book of the series! It's all about your personal life as a Youth Specialist. What could be more intriguing than that?